FREE PRIZE INSIDE!

Also by Seth Godin

Permission Marketing
Unleashing the Ideavirus
The Big Red Fez
Survival Is Not Enough
Purple Cow

Only in eBook Format

The Bootstrapper's Bible
What Should Google Do?
Really Bad PowerPoint
Bull Market

FREE PRIZE INSIDE!

THE NEXT BIG MARKETING IDEA

SETH GODIN

PORTFOLIO

PORTFOLIO
Published by the Penguin Group • Penguin Group (USA) Inc., 375 Hudson Street,
New York, New York 10014, U.S.A. • Penguin Books Ltd, 80 Strand, London
WC2R 0RL, England • Penguin Books Australia Ltd, 250 Camberwell Road,
Camberwell, Victoria 3124, Australia • Penguin Books Canada Ltd, 10 Alcorn
Avenue, Toronto, Ontario, Canada M4V 3B2 • Penguin Books India (P) Ltd,
11 Community Centre, Panchsheel Park, New Delhi – 110 017, India •
Penguin Books (N.Z.) Ltd, Cnr Rosedale and Airborne Roads, Albany, Auckland,
New Zealand • Penguin Books (South Africa) (Pty) Ltd, 24 Sturdee Avenue,
Rosebank, Johannesburg 2196, South Africa

Penguin Books Ltd, Registered Offices:
80 Strand, London WC2R 0RL, England

First published in 2004 by Portfolio,
a member of Penguin Group (USA) Inc.

10   9   8   7   6   5   4   3   2   1

Publisher's Note
This publication is designed to provide accurate and authoritative information in
regard to the subject matter covered. It is sold with the understanding that the
publisher is not engaged in rendering legal, accounting or other professional services.
If you require legal advice or other expert assistance, you should seek the services of a
competent professional.

Library of Congress Cataloging-in-Publication Data
Godin, Seth.
Free prize inside! : the next big marketing idea / Seth Godin.
p.   cm.
ISBN 1-59184-041-4
1. Marketing. I. Title.
HF5415.G577 2004
658.8—dc22   2003070688

This book is printed on acid-free paper. ∞

Printed in the United States of America
Set in Minion with Trade Gothic
Designed by Daniel Lagin

For Lynn and Rick

THE NEXT BIG MARKETING IDEA?

MAYBE NOT. MAYBE THIS IS JUST A BOOK ABOUT HOW EVERY SINGLE ONE OF US CAN CREATE IDEAS THAT MAKE OUR PRODUCTS AND SERVICES REMARKABLE.

It turns out that the people who make things happen—the champions—are now in short supply and more successful than ever. This is a book about a very simple idea (one that you've probably thought of yourself): If you make your product, your service, your school, your church or your career worth talking about, the word will spread. Go make something happen, and it'll pay off.

I bet you can do just that.

If you're lucky, your boss bought you this book. It's proof that your company wants you to do great things. On the other hand, maybe you should buy a copy of this book for your boss—and let her know that *you* really want to do great things.

This book is not just a management book. It's a book for individuals, managers *and* CEOs. That's because this book is a marketing book. *It's a marketing book for an era where the real marketing happens inside the product, not in the ad pages of a magazine.*

My goal is to sell you on taking on the challenge of doing the essential task of creating innovation. Not by building an organization that is automatically and effortlessly innovative—that's impossible. No, by creating a desire among individuals to do the work they must do to make innovation happen.

This is work that matters. Work that's worth doing. If I succeed in inspiring you to try, and then succeed in guiding you around some of the pitfalls, this book has been worth writing (and reading!).

Three Ways

If you want, turn to the end of the book (p. 235) and read the summary of *Free Prize Inside!* Then you can go back to the office and pretend you read the whole thing.

Or you can read the book that follows.

Or after you've read it through once, you can read it while referring to the dozens of pages of endnotes that start on p. 185. Then you'll really be an expert. The endnotes are also online, updated regularly, at www.freeprizeinside.com.

Enjoy.

ACKNOWLEDGMENTS

Helping someone with a book is not thankless, but it is a no-win proposition. Here are my selfless friends, allies and aides, who you should feel free to blame for anything in this book you don't like: Christopher Ireland at cheskin.com, Ramit Sethi at Stanford, Karen Watts, Robin Dellabough and especially Lisa DiMona at Lark. Adrian Zackheim, Will Weisser, Allison Sweet, Stephanie Land and Mark Ippoliti at Portfolio. Joseph Perez for the fabulous cover and the patience to live with the world's loudest backseat driver. Joi Ito and Heath Row in cyberspace and Dean Kamen on two wheels. Big thinkers like Andrew Beebe, Chris Meyer, Marcia Hart, Jackie Huba and Tim Manners. David Evenchick, Steve Dennis, Nancy Pellowe Dennis, Keith Yamashita, Chris Anderson and Jacqueline Novogratz for living out loud (and well). Jonathan Sackner Bernstein, for embodying the idea of the champion. Jerry Colonna, for never failing to find a good reason.

Helene, Alex and Mo: "Great idea! Write it down!" and for

the Wrigley story. My dad, Bill Godin, who is my hero and role model. Tom Cohen, for consistently being suave, smart and steadfast. Fred Hills, for setting a high standard. Yo-yoers David Simon, Jerry Shereshewsky, Dan Lovy, Barbara Johnson, Michael Landau and Mark Hurst for doing great stuff, with care. John Byrne, for picking up where Alan and Bill left off, and Alan and Bill for turning the volume up to 11.

Special hugs to Red Maxwell for making every single thing look good. Ann Shepherd for being my favorite elf, and Eve Yohalem for lunch. Mark Vamos never fails to improve my columns for *Fast Company* and Heath Row spreads them into cyberspace. Michael Cader always manages to execute something that's worth talking about—and he understands just how crazy this business is. Stuart Krichevsky is a beacon of rational entrepreneurship (and a great friend). Pam Dorman never fails to indulge my rants and raves.

Every day, I get a lot of e-mail. All of you who have shared your stories, your predicaments and your gratitude have made this journey a lot of fun. You are who this book is really for.

Thanks.

Seth Godin

seth@sethgodin.com

FREE PRIZE
INSIDE!

How Much Does a Paper Clip Cost?

Soon after I started my first company while in college, my partner laughed at me. I had announced to the office staff that we would save money by diligently reusing paper clips. "If we don't throw them out, there's no reason we should ever have to buy another box," I said, proudly lifting up the big box I had just purchased.

My partner pointed out that paper clips were so cheap as to be essentially free, and perhaps I'd be better off focusing my limited intellect on something more pressing. Basically, I was being an idiot by trying to save money on a cheap commodity.

Paper clips, however, didn't used to be so cheap.

There are dozens of patents for paper clips. At the turn of the last century, paper clip technology was a closely guarded secret. Hundreds of inventors were scrambling to invent a better paper clip.

This was soon followed by big-time advertising battles for paper clip market share. In 1910, when a stapler was a fancy piece of office equipment, advertising your brand of paper clip made a lot of sense.

Paper clip manufacturers were in search of a killing. And they knew they could make one by creating a better clip or by building a better brand.

In the paper clip parable, we see the two ideologies that every product that struggles not to be a commodity stands on:

● Build something no one else can build (so you can charge enough to make a profit)

● Advertise it like crazy to build a brand (so you can charge enough to make a profit)

If consumers were totally rational, advertising wouldn't work. Consumers would consider all the choices and buy the cheapest one or the one that has a noncopyable technical advantage. In a world like that, you'd either have a patent or process monopoly or you'd be selling your stuff at ultralow (no profit) prices.

But what fun is that?

Before you were born, marketers discovered that if they advertised like crazy, they could turn ad dollars into cash. They realized that they could differentiate their products without changing the products themselves. They discovered that they could charge better-than-commodity prices without creating a better-than-commodity product.

The reason paper clips are so cheap is that, a hundred years after they were invented, there's really no room for a major innovation in the way they're designed and produced. Without a technological edge, you've got nothing but a worthless commodity on your hands, something not worth much effort. The only way to make paper clips profitable, it seems, is to figure out some very cool branding and advertising that compels people to pay extra to buy your brand instead of another.

But most people, if you asked them, would tell you that they're not overly swayed by advertising, that they buy the right product at the right price for their company or home.

Of course, they don't. Until recently, they paid extra for truly effective advertising.

Until recently.

Remember Mr. Bubble?

Or Mrs. Butterworth's? Or Mr. Coffee?

There are plenty of products that used to be right there in the middle of our radar screen. Products with good profit margins, plenty of growth and lots of shelf space.

These products thrived because they were average. They were average products for average people—with great advertising. It was a great system: Every time the brand marketers spent

$100 on advertising and other forms of interruption, they made $200 in profit. They were marketing successfully to the masses, and were great at squeezing every dollar out of the process. They were able to charge noncommodity prices because they'd created a brand.

Today, twenty years later, it's easy for a marketer to get nostalgic about this. One product after another is fading away, for a simple reason: The ads can't pay for themselves anymore. Not only can't we make our paper clips profitable with advertising, it's getting difficult for vodkas, cars and accounting firms as well.

What we've learned is this: In an era of too much noise and too much clutter and too many choices and too many channels and too much spam, you can't make a good living by interrupting people over and over.

The TV-industrial complex, that graceful cycle that repaid advertisers with ever-increasing profits (which led to ever-increasing ad buys) seems to be crumbling.

Smart marketers started to flee—running from expensive mass media—as soon as they realized that building a brand using interruption media (advertising) is a loser's game, and now they're searching for something else.

Jeff Bezos Understands
That Advertising Is Dead

A year ago, Amazon.com announced that they were going to stop advertising altogether. No more TV. No more magazine ads. Instead, the company decided to put the money it was spending on ads into free shipping instead.

Marketers were aghast. The idea of investing your ad dollars into actually making the product better was heresy. Pundits once again proclaimed the death of Amazon.

After twelve months, the results were in. Sales for the year were up 37 percent. International growth was an astonishing 81 percent. Amazon reported its first quarterly nonholiday profit, attributed to growth due to the change in marketing tactics.

Jeff Bezos and his shareholders are thriving by abandoning the TV-industrial complex. They reject the idea that they have to interrupt people with ads they don't want to get. They reject the notion that the only way to build sustainable competitive advantage in a nontechnology industry is to have ever more clever ads, reaching ever more annoyed consumers.

The list of companies that have recorded record growth without heavy dependence on the TV-industrial complex continues to expand. Meetup grew to more than half a million users without running an ad. The Dyson vacuum cleaner continues to break sales records—without obscene ad spending.

Wi-Fi has become the de facto standard for wireless Internet connectivity, for a tiny fraction of the money wasted by much better funded competitors.

> Just because you have money doesn't mean you can trade it for attention by buying advertising. Consumers have learned how to ignore you.

Red Lobster, on the Other Hand . . .

When you think of the Red Lobster restaurant chain, do you think of their new slogan, Share the Love? According to Gary Epstein, chief executive at Euro RSCG Tatham Partners, "This campaign really captures kind of the heart and soul of what people feel about both the brand and about eating seafood." Huh?

Red Lobster is so sure that their new spin on their old restaurants will be effective that they've announced a $60 million ad campaign. Sixty million dollars interrupting people with messages they don't want to get about a restaurant they've already heard of.

Of course, it's not really Red Lobster's fault.

All around us, we're seeing the symptoms of the failing TV-industrial complex, but many companies don't seem to be reacting to the decreased effectiveness of advertising as a tool to rapidly grow their business. Why?

Because the marketing department doesn't get a lot of

choice. The marketing department gets a budget and a few tools. Those tools are things like ads, coupons and rebates. Given their mission and the tools available to them, it's not surprising that they run ads—it's all they've got. It takes guts to say to your boss, "Let's stop running ads and start making a re-markable product instead."

Marketing Matters, and It's All Marketing

In *Purple Cow*, I tried to show you how being remarkable is the shortcut to growth. The goal of this book is to go much further. I want to expand the realm of marketing, and to persuade you and your peers that *everyone in the company is in the marketing department.*

> Here's the quick definition of a Purple Cow: A Purple Cow is a product or service that's remarkable. "Re-markable" simply means that a customer is willing to make a remark about it. If you can create remarkable products, people will talk about them. If that happens, the word will spread and your sales will grow. That explains the success of most every fast-growing company of the last ten years.
>
> Are you invisible? Or remarkable?

If your goal is growth, marketing is all that matters—and everything you do is now part of marketing.

If marketing is about communicating to consumers that you've solved their problem, then the first step is, in fact, to solve their problem. In our ever-more networked world, if you do that well enough, the communication part of the equation is easier to solve.

> Every product and every service can be made remarkable. And anyone in your organization can make it happen.

Can I Get It, Mom?

If you were like me, you nagged your mom to buy the cereal with the free prize inside. You bought Cracker Jacks to get the goofy little prize, too. We may have known that the cereal without a prize was just as good, but of course, it wasn't just as good. It didn't have a prize.

In those days, cereal makers had it easy. They could offer a free prize *and* create amazing advertising as well. They could charge a significant premium over the generic brands if they had a talking tiger or a toucan or a Cap'n riding a boat through a sea of milk.

Today, of course, that's no longer true. Cereal isn't the cash machine it used to be, there are too many brands, not enough shelf space and a newly cost-sensitive consumer that isn't fooled by TV advertising.

All we've got left is the prize. The only way to stand out and command noncommodity pricing is to innovate. You can innovate with a licensed character or a cool shape or high-protein ingredients. You can innovate with packaging or pricing or even—yes, it's true—by putting a cool prize in the box.

It's not only cereal. More than a decade ago, when Lincoln-Mercury started putting Bose stereos in their high-end cars, they were astonished to discover that more than half the buyers opted to add the $8,000 stereo to their $12,000 cars. The amazing thing is that almost none of these people had a stereo even remotely that expensive in their living rooms at home. They thought they were going out to buy a car, but they were entranced by something else—the innovation, the free prize. They were buying a stereo with wheels.

Innovation Is Actually Cheaper Than Advertising

It didn't used to be true, but in a world of Purple Cows, when the marketing is built into the product, creating products that are innovative is actually cheaper than advertising average products.

So, once your company realizes (and is sold on) that insight, then it will invest the money it would have spent on advertising to create cool products instead. That innovation is free. In fact, it's a profit center.

Big companies don't blink before spending $100 million on

the marketing for a product launch. Small companies spend plenty on billboards or local advertising. But since that isn't working, they'd be better off spending half that amount and making something really special instead.

By the time you finish this book, you'll discover that the future belongs to companies, organizations and people who are remarkable, not boring.

Introducing the Godin Curve

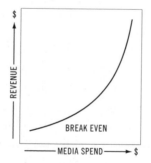

The right half of the curve demonstrates that as you invest in media, you need to have a higher and higher expected return to break even. That makes sense. If you run a ton of Super Bowl ads or spend a lot of time and money to get on *Oprah*, that's expensive. It's a risk. You need a big payoff to make it worth it.

I'm not making a controversial assertion here. The simple

fact is that the more you spend, the more sales you need to justify that spending (and the risk and overhead that goes with it).

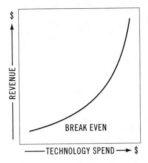

The left part of the curve shows that the same is true for technology. If you spend a fortune building a gizmo, you need to have a very high expected return in order to break even on your investment and have enough left over to have the risk of the investment be worth it.

When Iridium invested $3 billion to launch sixty-six satellites in permanent orbit around the Earth, they were making a very big bet. In order to make a bet like that pay off, the return has to be astronomical.

The Godin curve combines the two parts, then adds a dotted line. The dotted line shows how much revenue you can expect (historically) from big investments in media or technology. Yes, you generate more revenue when you get a big ad campaign right or when you launch a high-tech success. Surprisingly, though, the increase in revenue isn't commensurate with the in-

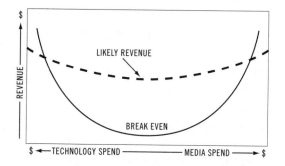

crease in risk. You can spend more and more, but you can't earn more and more.

Big technology and media projects rarely generate the huge returns necessary to make them worth the effort. Sometimes they fail altogether. Iridium went bankrupt. So did Pets.com. Even when they do work, they often generate relatively little more revenue than cheaper campaigns or cheaper technology do.

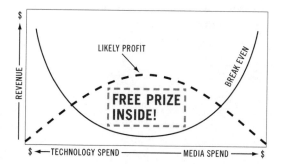

The final version of the curve (named after Antoine Godin, the great explorer) subtracts the costs of development and media from the project's revenue and shows your likely profit (the dotted line). The spot between the two curves is the free-prize zone, the place where a different kind of innovation lives, the place where *you* can live and work and profit.

Let me make it really clear:

- You can't afford difficult and risky technological innovation, because the return you'll receive is unlikely to justify the investment.

- You can't afford to do huge media and PR buys because the return you'll receive is unlikely to justify the investment.

But you *can* profit all day long by leveraging insight and creativity to come up with cheap innovations that have a significant return. The center of the curve is all yours.

> Huge returns go to organizations that create remarkable innovations, regardless of their cost or provenance.

WHY YOU NEED A FREE PRIZE ✹ 15

How Can This Be?

This is counterintuitive. It implies that the things that "smart" (big) companies have been spending the most on is the stuff that doesn't really matter.

Exactly.

Each incremental dollar on big ad spending doesn't contribute appropriate incremental profit in return.

Each incremental dollar spent on big R&D and technology investment doesn't contribute appropriate incremental profit in return.

The two pillars have crumbled. Differentiating yourself with patents or ads is too hard. Something else is at work. There's a new way of winning, and it's happening because of a confluence of reinforcing events.

1. Consumers (at home or at work) have always wanted more than they say they want. We proclaim ourselves to be rational, cost-conscious, *Consumer Reports*–reading smart people. In fact, we are happy to pay extra for whitewall tires, beautiful leather nappiness on our shoes, a sophisticated showroom in which to shop and even stamps we don't have to lick. We don't insist on the biggest ads or the latest technology. We want cool stuff.

    Design matters. Style matters. Extras matter. We want the free prize, sometimes more than we want the thing itself.

J. D. Power announced in 2003 that Land Rover was near the bottom of their customer service index ranking, right near Kia, Isuzu and Daewoo. This doesn't seem to have any effect on their sales, which are at record levels. Apparently, people are buying Land Rovers at a huge premium over most any other car, even though the main thing a car is *supposed* to do—run when you want it to run—isn't one of its strong points. It's the design and the look and the legend and brochure and the dealership, and the look in your neighbor's eye when you drive it home. Obviously, people are buying the car for some reason that does not have much to do with going from one place to another.

2. We now live in a world where the path from great idea to the consumer is shorter than ever. It used to take years to build a plant, set up distribution, do the advertising and get the product into the hands of the user. The rules have changed. Within four hours of Arnold Schwarzenegger's surprise announcement about his gubernatorial bid, someone was selling T-shirts with his image online. This means that there's less reason to build some giant campaign for the future— the competition is building something for *right now.*

3. The tools that are available to creators are so much better than they used to be. We can prototype machines on our desktop, mock up Web sites on our desktop, and even model behaviors on our desktop. The bar for truly revolutionary technical innovation keeps getting higher. Getting a world-

beating patent isn't something you can do in your basement anymore. You need a lot of money and a lot of time.

Because we're less open to the big and the slow (and very responsive to the clever and the quick), the return on being big and slow isn't what it used to be.

> The half-life of a successful product is shorter than ever, so ideas need to be cheaper to build and faster to market.

Living (and Thriving) in the Free Prize Zone

The obvious lesson from the Godin curve is that the place to spend your time, your money and your career is in the center of the curve. That creating the innovations that people pay for is actually a profitable venture—it's not a cost center, it's free.

There are challenges, of course. Most companies aren't organized to do this. Most individuals aren't trained to pursue it. And most people haven't been sold on why it's important.

This book addresses all three stumbling blocks. My goal is to cajole you into stepping into this zone and investing the energy it takes to revolutionize your products—and make them remarkable.

Soft Innovation Is Innovation Anyone Can Do

Most writing on innovation is about paradigm shifts, big projects, huge R&D and technical changes. It's about nanotechnology and space farming.

Most successes, though, are actually the result of what I'll call soft innovation. Stuff like fast lube job shops, cell phone pricing plans and purple ketchup.

What really works? No surprise, it's the soft stuff. The commonsense, creative stuff that requires initiative and curiosity, not an advanced degree, to do.

The reason soft innovation works is that all breakthroughs (big and small) require quantum leaps. It's much easier, of course, to take a quantum leap with style or insight or guts (a nontechnical breakthrough) than it is by toying with the rules of physics or jumping Moore's curve.

Please don't misunderstand me. I'm eternally grateful to Edison for inventing the lightbulb and Salk for perfecting the polio vaccine. These were heavy-duty breakthroughs that involved equal parts of persistence and genius. If you're hot on the trail of a quantum breakthrough in your technical field, please proceed!

My message is aimed at everyone else. It's aimed at everyone who's been told that they're not qualified, authorized or entitled to pursue breakthroughs of any kind, that they must pursue the status quo while waiting for R&D to deliver the latest insight and marketing to come up with the next great ad campaign (Share the Love anyone?).

Quick Definitions: A **soft innovation** is what *you,* the marketer, see. If it catches on and becomes something the *consumer* wants, it is now a free prize.

A **free prize** is the essence of a Purple Cow. Generally, a free prize has two key characteristics. First, it's the thing about your service, your product or your organization that's worth remarking on, something worth seeking out and buying. (Alas, most soft innovations never become free prizes, because most soft innovations aren't remarkable.) Second, a free prize is not about what a person needs. Instead, it satisfies our wants. It is fashionable or fun or surprising or delightful or sad. It rarely delivers *more* of what we were buying in the first place. It delivers something extra.

A product or service that carries a free prize is a **Purple Cow**.

The Surgeon and the Nurse

I had hernia surgery. It costs a lot, it hurts and the hospital makes a fortune.

The places it hurts might surprise you. The surgery gives you a very sore throat, because they clamp your mouth open while you're asleep. It also hurts a lot when you pee, because they use a catheter.

The surgeon doesn't care one bit about how much it hurts.

He's a superhero, he cuts and sews and moves on. But the hospital cares. The hospital cares because they know that most patients have a choice when it comes to ambulatory surgery, and that choice is dictated in large measure by how positive the word of mouth from other patients is.

The traditional way for a hospital to improve its services is with technological innovation. Buying million-dollar MRI machines or investing in a huge new facility. But that ignores free prize thinking.

As I lay in the recovery room for two hours, all I could think about was how much my throat hurt and how difficult it was to pee. The surgeon told me later that this happens to everyone. He told me that if I had gulped down some cranberry juice and sucked on a throat lozenge when I got home, I would have had a much easier time.

So here's the question: Why didn't someone offer me a throat lozenge and a glass of cranberry juice at the hospital? Some dietician had decided that apple juice and graham crackers were the right thing to offer to recovering patients, and that was that. The nurses, good at following instructions, were following these rules as well.

But what if one brave nurse had the guts to ask a surgeon if she could offer a Sucret and a glass of cranberry juice instead? How much would that innovation cost?

The return on investment is huge. Charging $5,000 a patient

for half a day, all the hospital needs to do is get one or two new surgeries a year as a result of word of mouth to pay for a lifetime supply of Sucrets. It's really simple: The nurse could have created a soft innovation—something useful and magical and thoughtful—that might have become a free prize. Only when you find the free prize will your customers start to talk about you.

I Wish Highway 11 Were Beautiful, but It's Not

Highway 11 is the road taken by thousands of people every day as they travel from Toronto to some of the most stunning country I've ever seen. Crystal-clear lakes, awe-inspiring moose and millions of trees.

But along the way, you've got to pass gas stations, junk shops, fireworks stores, more gas stations, doughnut shops, coffee shops and abandoned wild blueberry stands. In one three-kilometer stretch, it's possible to pass at least three vivid examples of each of these, all jammed together in one endless, mind-numbing strip.

Then, around the bend, next to a famous hamburger stand, you'll find Rita's. Her store doesn't even have a name. The sign out front says, CANDY SHOPPE.

Over the last four years, Rita's candy shop has been one of

the fastest-growing stores in the entire country. Rita has recorded annual sales increases of close to 100 percent and had some months where sales go up 50 percent from the month before. She's done all this by building a Purple Cow.

Nearly everything about the store is remarkable. Rita sells candy that you can't get anywhere else in the country. She sells individually wrapped bags of penny candy so you don't have to worry about some kid's grimy hands. She sells flavors and brands that you remember from your childhood but thought were gone forever. She even sells spotted dick, the infamous British pudding in a can.

The average customer spends $30 to $100, depending on the season. $100 worth of candy!

It's pretty easy to look at this business and realize that nearly anyone could have started it. Rita is personable and hardworking and she loves her products, but she's not the only shopkeeper in Canada who could run this store. So, the question I want to answer is this: Why Rita?

Why is Rita the only one doing something so remarkable? Why is it so easy to get your friends, family, neighbors and even bankers to support your effort to open yet another doughnut shop, but so wonderfully rare to find someone running a shop as cool (and successful) as Rita's?

In the world of the Purple Cow, where the product *is* the marketing, the winners are the people able to champion remarkable ideas and make them happen. And the astonishing revelation is this: Innovation isn't just fun, it's free. It doesn't take rare skill or astonishing talent. It doesn't have to involve huge expenditures of time and money. And the innovations you create will have a far faster (and bigger) payback than the more ordinary stuff you're spending so much time and effort on.

TEN SOFT INNOVATIONS ANYONE COULD HAVE DONE

Every one of these ten ideas is a free prize. Every one transformed an ordinary organization or product into a remarkable one, a Purple Cow worth talking about. And every one could have been conceived by someone like you.

Three Dog Bakery: purveyor of food for dogs that contains 100-percent natural, people-grade ingredients. "This store wasn't for the pets, of course. It was for the owners. It's theater," says Ann Willoughby, who helped create the chain of more than twenty-five stores around the world.

Prehistoric pasta: Twenty years ago, Chef Boyardee introduced dinosaurs to the world of kids' food. They created a sensation, generating millions of dollars' worth of incremental sales of canned macaroni (in the shape of *Tyrannosaurus Rex,* in fact). One problem: The National Academy of Sciences criticized Chef Boyardee for getting the number of claws on the *T. rex* wrong. They fixed it.

Saving lives, saving money: Dr. Peter Pronovost realized that doctors kill more than 98,000 patients a year because they fail to follow simple steps. One Sunday night, he invented a simple checklist for doctors, and started using it the next day. In studies, his checklist has been shown to decrease the average stay in the intensive care ward by 50 percent.

PowerBar: Yes, they've been around since 1986. And anyone who saw that athletes wanted a food to eat before, during or after exercising could have invented this multibillion-dollar product category.

Portable shredding: bakery-truck-size rolling shredding machines. They drive up to a business, take its confidential documents, shred them and drive off.

Endless Pools: treadmills for swimmers. Tens of thousands are installed in gyms and homes around the world.

The 52 Deck Series: Lynn Gordon developed beautifully illustrated little gift books. Except they're not gift books. They're decks of cards with text and pictures offering fifty-two great ideas for what to do on a rainy day, or on a visit to New York City, or even if you can't sleep. Sales so far? More than five million decks.

The iPod: You can spend half as much on a competitor and get space to hold even more music. What you can't get is the beautiful industrial design and the effortless user interface. People aren't buying a hard disk in a box. They're buying the free prize that comes from the satisfaction you get from using it.

QBNet: fast barbershops in Japan. Get a cut in one-sixth the time and for one-quarter the price. They've grown from 57,000 cuts a year in 1996 to more than 3.5 million haircuts in 2002.

The Swatch: At the peak of this brand's frenzy, a Swatch sold at auction for more than $20,000. The idea behind this mammoth brand is simple: cheap Swiss watches with great fashion sense. Watches worth talking about, watches worth collecting. Before Swatch, only millionaires collected watches.

Innovation Envy Gets Us Sidetracked

It glides and floats and spins and soars. Everyone who sees it wants to touch it and talk about it and take it for a ride. It's a remarkable innovation.

Dean Kamen, the inventor, is one in a million. He revolutionized the wheelchair, dialysis machines and the way African villages make clean water. Now he's trying to change the way we walk around. I think he's a genius and I'm glad to know him.

But the Segway represents everything that's wrong with the way we think about innovation. The Segway cost more than $80 million to develop. The project was a crapshoot the entire time—no one was ever sure if it was going to function as designed or not. The Segway was built by highly trained, brilliant engineers, the kind of rocket scientists we might be proud to know, but not people like us.

Worse, the Segway required that an entirely new company be formed to get it off the ground. It involved building a new marketing effort and a major hype and sales rollout in order to generate enough sales to make it worth the journey.

The Segway is the kind of bet-the-company, high-risk innovation we all dream about. It's the big fat audacious innovation that (when it works) becomes legendary. But the Segway was expensive and the Segway took years to develop.

That's not the kind of innovation I want to talk about. I love the Segway and I'm glad Dean built it, but I think there's another way. I think there are *free* innovations waiting for *you* to roll them out.

The Price of "Wow" Keeps on Rising

That was the headline in *The New York Times*. And they're right. Using a technology breakthrough or a nationwide ad campaign to get people to say wow is not as easy as it used to be. When Hollywood turned the Terminator into molten metal, people said wow. The same level of wow in *The Matrix* cost five or ten times as much.

The first time we saw a blimp at a football game, we said wow. Now, we don't even notice it (was it Fuji or Goodrich?

Goodyear?). Once you've been wowed, the same trick doesn't work anymore. Once we've seen a clever advertising joke or played with a cool new technology, they don't deliver the same wow the next time. Which is why using the expensive, heavy-hitter techniques is way too expensive.

CD Baby Is a Purple Cow

Derek Sivers is a smart guy, but he's not a geek. He's a musician.

A few years ago, in the midst of the dot-com boom, Derek had an idea for an online company that would sell CDs from unsigned, self-published musicians. If he had gone to a venture capital firm, they would have insisted he hire high-priced technical minds to build a vast and proprietary system, a defensible technology. Then they would have piled on the marketing money, helping him build a brand footprint that would be impregnable for years to come, giving him time to pay off the costs of the technology. Then, of course, he would have gone bankrupt.

Instead, Derek taught himself how to use FileMaker. In a few months, he built a simple but elegant system that would let him run his business online. And then he spent the rest of his time building soft innovations that would attract artists, consumers and profits.

This chart of increasing commissions to musicians demonstrates CD Baby's results:

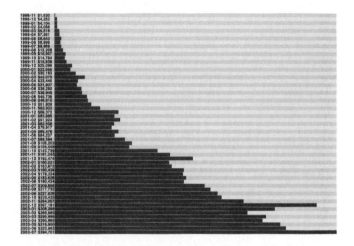

While other dot-coms have come and gone, Derek is doing great. He's winning because of the design of the site, the
musician-friendly policies, the funny e-mails and his management skills. He's winning because instead of spending time and
money on R&D and media, he's spending insight and creativity
on the free prize.

Getting Rid of a Problem
Is As Good As Adding a Feature

As you may know, Amtrak invested more than $800 million in
building the high-speed Acela train. It runs from Boston to
Washington, D.C., and it really is a wonder. It's faster and easier

than the airplane, yet they're having a lot of trouble persuading people who take the short shuttle flight to Washington from New York to switch.

The company has taken two tacks to make the business work. The first is to run a ton of advertising, hoping to interrupt their way to success.

The second is to invest in hugely expensive trains and to install automated ticket machines at the stations to make it similar to taking a plane.

And today, because they don't understand the power of soft innovation, I almost missed my train.

It seems that the automated ticket machines haven't been programmed to allow a walk-on passenger to buy a ticket in the hour before a train leaves. Of course, that's precisely when you would expect that a walk-on passenger would *want* to buy a ticket. Instead, after you've pressed all the buttons, the machine says, "We are having problems processing your ticket, please see an agent."

So, I went to see the agent. But the wait for the agent (there's only one working at a time—they alternate, apparently) lasts for more than half an hour. With four minutes left before the train departs and no sign of the front of the line, I panic. I pick up my cell phone and call Amtrak. The kind woman on the other end puts in my reservation, then I walk over to the machine and less than thirty seconds later, I have my ticket.

I went back to the line and announced to the other twenty

nervous people about to miss their train how they can make a call and do a work-around on the machine. They all scurry off and make their train.

Of course, if we had all missed our train, how likely would we have been to choose Amtrak next time? Amtrak had spent a fortune building a Purple Cow, and a tiny technical glitch was powerful enough to undo all of it.

Obviously, the return on investment of fixing this problem is huge. But how to fix it without another huge investment in technology or staffing?

How about a simple handwritten sign on a three-by-five card, posted at the entrance to the interminable line. It could give the phone number of Amtrak along with instructions on how to make the machine dispense a ticket!

By getting rid of the problem that made Amtrak *not* like the airlines, one employee could have created a chance for the railroad to spread the word.

A free prize. Just waiting for someone to grab it.

> Fix what's broken.

Are Supermodels a Gimmick— or What People Really Want?

People have the same sort of sneering disdain for the word "gimmick" that they have for "used car salesman." A gimmick is cheap, a trick, a ruse, something not worth the time or attention of a professional.

I think we need to take another look.

Were frequent-flier miles a gimmick? When they came out, most people treated them that way. After all, flying was about getting from place to place, not earning points and winning prizes. Today, American Airlines understands that their frequent-flier program is one of their great assets.

Is product design a gimmick? If we need a music player or a car or a teapot, shouldn't we focus on the way the thing works, not the way it makes us feel? Well, unless you're driving a used Yugo and listening to an old Aiwa cassette player, I think you've already voted with your dollars.

What about the comics in your local newspaper? I mean, you read it for news, right? If you had a choice between reading a newspaper without color photos (which, ostensibly, deliver the news in a more powerful way) or a newspaper without comics (a circulation gimmick, after all), which would you choose?

William Wrigley's company started out selling soap. As an extra incentive for merchants to carry their soap, they offered stores free baking powder with every purchase. When baking powder proved to be more popular than soap, they stopped making soap and started selling baking powder. Then Wrigley got the idea to offer merchants free chewing gum with each can of baking powder. A gimmick?

I think a gimmick needs to be defined as a feature that the consumer might be attracted to but doesn't really want. Something that doesn't help them solve a problem, even if the problem isn't the main reason they're buying the item in the first place. A gimmick is only a gimmick when it is noise, a distraction, something that takes away from the item itself.

We can't know if a gimmick is a gimmick forever (like the sock glue they sell in Japan to hold up the high socks the teenagers love) or a gimmick for a little while (like the prize in the Cracker Jack box). Once a gimmick becomes something that consumers want and something that consumers talk about—the prize in the Cracker Jack box—it stops being a gimmick. And the only way to find out is to try it. The marketplace decides, not you.

The gimmick transformed, the soft innovation, that's what we're here for. We buy what we want, not what we need, and we want soft innovations.

> If it satisfies consumers and gets them to tell other people what you want them to tell other people, it's not a gimmick. It's a soft innovation.

Prodigy Built Technology
and AOL Built a Free Prize

Prodigy was founded by Sears, IBM and CBS. They spent several billion dollars building the company. I once visited one of their underground, earthquake-proof server buildings (they were building them nationwide). They installed high-tech security devices (with photo badges) years before I saw them anywhere else except in spy movies. If it was hardware, they had it.

Steve Case built AOL using the cheapest computers he could find. It crashed a lot. There were busy signals. There were always growing pains at AOL, but never at Prodigy.

Yet Jan Brandt, the marketing whiz who helped build AOL, understood that giving away free floppy disks (and then CDs) in every venue she could find was worth more than buying fancy computers. She discovered that the "gimmick" of free hours and easy installation was actually the very thing that people had been waiting for. Prodigy lost, because they believed in serious R&D. They sold the company for pennies on the dollar. AOL won with a soft innovation that anyone could have invented.

> Do people want the fortune cookie or the fortune?

Soft Innovations Keep Showing Up

Robert A. Moon was a regional executive at the Postal Service when he invented the zip code. An unbelievably simple idea—that has saved postal customers billions of dollars.

Murray Pergament owned a hardware store on Long Island when he saw the huge growth of the suburbs—and realized that all those people in all those houses were going to need to buy a lot of stuff. In 1946, he began to build the profitable Pergament superstore chain, long before Home Depot popularized home improvement superstores.

In an hour, Lester Wunderman created hundreds of millions of dollars' worth of value for the Columbia House Music Club. Not by building a new distribution facility or buying a ton of TV ads. He did it by inventing the "little gold box" that they mentioned on their TV ads. This innovation, all by itself, enabled Columbia House to run twenty years of profitable direct-response TV ads.

The market for vitamins was small and stagnant until Flintstones vitamins came along. Chewing on Wilma and Dino isn't a gimmick as far as kids are concerned—it's the only reason to take one!

Sixty years ago, Robert de Graff invented the paperback book. A simple idea, yet one that was met with a huge amount of resistance—from the publishing industry, not consumers.

The public loved the idea, and it led to literally billions of books being sold.

Lucille Roberts didn't have a lot of money or know much about building exercise machines. But she did understand that not just rich people wanted to work out. By stripping her gyms of all amenities and packing in machinery, she made a workout affordable for working women. When she died, she had dozens of clubs in operation.

Brownie Wise created a business bigger than one hundred Segways—she invented the Tupperware party. Of course, she started with a great product, but her ability to see beyond her job title and invent a whole new way of selling (the home party) was the company's single greatest innovation. Brownie figured out that the way kitchen storage products were sold was as important as the way they were made.

The Four Seasons restaurant in Manhattan made even jaded New Yorkers gasp when it opened in 1959. There, on the wall of the beautiful dining room, was a huge painting. An original Picasso. They don't just serve food at the Four Seasons. They guarantee an experience worth paying for.

Alan Webber and Bill Taylor started with the very same tools as every other magazine founder—two Macs, a telephone and access to a printer. Yet the magazine they started, *Fast Company*, was exceptional. It won the National Magazine Award. It grew like a weed. It changed people's lives. The investors sold it for more than $400 million. They won because they were remarkable—not because of great advertising (they had none) or because of wonderful technology (it was an ordinary magazine).

G.I. Joe appears to be a doll for boys. But dolls for boys never sold well. The free prize is how well the joints on a G.I. Joe articulate. By turning a doll into a legitimate action figure, Hasbro figured out how to breathe life into plastic.

The Uline industrial supplies catalog offers hard hats for construction workers—the standard kind, which costs $7, as well as the official NFL-licensed football-team-logo models, at $29. It doesn't matter whether you're selling to business, to education, to government or to consumers—products that have a free prize thrive.

Soft Innovation Works—Everywhere

The magic of the examples above is that ordinary people, using ordinary tools, were able to create products or services that generated both user satisfaction and profits. In any industry where people decide, style matters.

The opportunity here isn't subtle: Whatever you do, wherever you do it, you have the opportunity to create this sort of innovation. You have the power to find and develop a free prize.

Inflame the passionate.

A Free Prize Always Fades

If Krispy Kreme didn't exist, I'd probably have to invent it! The remarkable story behind their doughnuts was a big part of my last book, *Purple Cow*. But in 2004, less than a year later, it's reported that the guest count (a key measure of retailer health) at one large group of their stores is down by almost 20 percent over the last year.

No free prize lasts forever, which is why it's so essential that we get better at making new ones.

This Isn't Just a Book About Making Money, Though

It's my passionate belief that when teams of people get together and make something amazing, useful, helpful, productive, funny, inspiring or remarkable, we're at our full potential as humans.

That may sound sappy, but it's true. Monet was an artist, and so is the team that created the iPod. Building Purple Cows, and creating the soft innovations that turn into free prizes, isn't just a corporate priority—it's personal.

It's important. It's powerful and something you need to do. Satisfied businesspeople (and nonbusinesspeople, for that matter) are happy because they're actually *doing* something. They're building and creating and designing and leading and shaping and making something come to life.

I think the challenge (and the imperative) is to do something that matters. And more often than not, you'll find that the stuff that matters involves creating something new and remarkable.

Most of the work behind soft innovations is done in teams. A vibrant team can create an experience you'll remember forever.

1984 Wasn't Like 1984 . . .

Two cool things happened to me in 1984. First, Apple introduced the Macintosh. Here was a technological tour de force that also made the user feel powerful, excited and filled with possibility. Second was my opportunity to lead the team that built a suite of computer games at Spinnaker Software.

While many of the people on the team were engineers, only a few were brilliant nerds, unable to survive in the outside world. The rest of us were focused on how to share our vision of what the next generation of computer games would be like. We worked twenty hours a day, shipping five products in five months—a project that should have taken two or three years.

Do you know that I still hear from many members of that team? Twenty years later, many of us consider it one of the high points of our careers. It was exciting and essential and vibrant. Filling out forms and editing advertising copy pales in comparison.

> You owe it to yourself to create something remarkable
> one day.

Is Your Job Just a Job?

Your days can seem really long (and your life can seem really short) if you're spending your entire career wasting time merely to make some money.

Being engaged at work is seductive. It means that you're spending a big chunk of every day doing something you love, something that makes a difference. You get to motivate other people and create things that last. Unfortunately, this sort of opportunity is scarce and (apparently) getting even more scarce. The gift I can give you is this: Since your boss hired you to make something happen, you now have permission to build a free prize. You have the opportunity (on your boss's nickel) to build a project that will energize you and your co-workers.

You Can Do It

The biggest insight about soft innovation is that anyone can do it. It's not based on your power in an organization, or your desire to become an entrepreneur or how creative you are. My goal is to sell you on your ability to champion an innovation in your organization. To find a Purple Cow and a team to build it. And then to do it again and again.

Remember that inventing something and making it happen are not the same thing. You don't have to do the work to champion it. But your idea (all by itself) will fail unless *you* make it happen. This is a book about both steps of the process—creating an innovation and then causing it to happen—and you can't have one without the other.

Wait!

If You've Been Paying Attention . . .

You may have seen the problem. It's the problem that every company has and it's the problem that plagues my entire argument.

My argument so far:

1. Advertising doesn't work so well, because you can't buy attention.

2. Big R&D hardware innovations don't work so well, because they're so risky and ever more expensive.

3. Soft innovations are the sweet spot, the free prize, the means that will allow your organization to grow and thrive.

4. Anyone, including you, can create a successful soft innovation, even (and especially) if you're not in the marketing department.

5. Not only is it profitable, but it's empowering, engaging and fun.

So, you may be wondering, if this is so effective and so productive and requires so little training, *why doesn't everyone do it?* Exactly.

The Reasons Everyone Doesn't Do It

They're scared.

They're organized to resist change of any kind.

They don't understand that soft innovation isn't risky, it's free and important.

They don't realize how much their bosses want them to pursue soft innovations.

They've never been sold on doing it, and they've never been taught how to do it well.

This Means There's Huge Opportunity

Sometimes it's hard to imagine that there's still room to innovate your product or service. While it seems like the world is changing faster and faster, that everything that can be done *has* been done, that's not true. It turns out that there's a huge amount of inertia left in almost every category.

Every product, every service, every feature and every benefit is open for improvement. There's nothing that's finished, nothing so complete that it can't carry another free prize. No, not carry a prize ... be transformed by a prize, transformed so completely that the product category finds new life.

The shift from hard stuff (big technology and big media) to the free prize is an ever-increasing spiral. When someone figures out how to create a new free prize, and to make yet another Purple Cow, the entire industry has to take notice. The cycle begins again, and continues to accelerate—and in almost every industry, that cycle is beginning, not ending.

Because your competition is petrified, rooted to their seats in fear, you've got an unfair advantage. You can create soft innovations faster, easier and with glee.

Henry Ford's Bargain: The Source of Our Fear

Henry Ford left us much more than cars and the highway system we built for them. He changed the world's expectations of work. While Ford gets credit for inventing the assembly line, his great insight was that he understood the power of productivity.

Ford was a pioneer in highly leveraged, repetitive work done by relatively untrained workers. A farmer, with little training, could walk into Ford's factory and become extraordinarily productive in a day or two.

This is the cornerstone of our way of life. The backbone of our economy is not brain surgeons and master violinists. It's fairly average people doing fairly average work.

The focus on productivity wouldn't be relevant to this discussion if not for another of Ford's innovations. He decided to pay his workers based on productivity, not replacement value. This was an astonishing breakthrough. When Ford announced the $5 day (more than double the typical salary paid to a similarly skilled factory worker), more than ten thousand people applied for work at Ford *the very next day.*

Instead of paying people the lowest amount necessary to find enough competent workers to fill the plant, he paid them *more* than he needed to because his system made them so productive. Then he challenged his workers to be even more productive so that they'd get paid even more.

It meant that nearly every factory worker at Ford was dramatically overpaid! When there's a line of people out the door waiting to take your job, weird things happen to your head. The combination of repetitive factory work *plus* high pay for standardized performance led to a very obedient factory floor. People were conditioned to do as they were told, and traded autonomy and craftsmanship for high pay and stability.

All of a sudden, we got used to being paid based on our output. We came, over time, to expect to get paid more and more, regardless of how long the line of people eager to take our jobs was. If productivity went up, profits went up. And the productive workers expected (and got) higher pay, even if there were plenty of replacement workers eager to work for less.

This is the central conceit of our economy. People in productive industries get paid a lot even though they could likely be replaced by someone else working for less money. This is why we're insecure.

Obedience works fine on the well-organized, standardized factory floor. But what happens when we start using our heads, not our hands, and our collars change from blue to white?

White-Collar Workers Don't Get Paid to Follow Instructions

The big difference between today and Ford's day is that instead of working with a drill or an arc welder, we work with laptops and telephones.

What's neat about this work is that it's different every day. We actually get a lot of freedom to decide what to do next, and our skill in making that decision has a lot to do with our productivity.

That's why your boss allows you the time to read this book or shop online or go to lunch meetings. Because she's waiting for you to break the rules and create big gains in productivity by using your head.

Yes, there are exceptions. There are clerks who have every keystroke timed and measured. But that's not really a white-collar job—that's a factory job where you don't get dirty. (You get carpal tunnel instead.)

I'm talking about the vast majority of jobs in our organizations, schools, governments and corporations. You don't have to wear a shop apron and you're expected to contribute more than what's being asked.

The thing is, because white-collar workers realize, deep down, that Henry Ford's principle is still at work, they're petrified to do exactly what it is they actually got hired to do—be different. We all know that we could get replaced tomorrow by someone almost as good who is willing to work for half as much money. We don't want to blow it. We want to be given instructions—not to invent them. After all, we know how to follow instructions!

We invented the myth that doing what your boss says is the best way to keep your job. In a white-collar setting, this isn't the right answer. Nine times out of ten, a white-collar worker's reflex is to ask, "What do *you* think I should do?" The easiest way to avoid pain, it seems, is to follow someone else's lead. That's why all the business magazines trot out the latest great leaders— it's what the working people think they need.

So, here's the paradox of the free prize. Creating innovations

is easy and profitable and productive and it's what we're supposed to do. *But* because we happen to like our jobs, we intentionally screw up the very system that hired us.

> The harder you try to play it safe, the more likely you
> are to fail.

You Can Wreck the Factory Where You Work by Following Instructions

We've fooled ourselves into thinking that white-collar work is
supposed to be as repetitive and rule-based as running a punch
press. So we often fight the innovators in our midst, pushing
back on those who would have us change and innovate and
push ourselves to do new stuff.

Think hard for a second about why that's a very bad idea.

If you worked at a General Motors plant and started wrecking punch presses by pouring oil all over them, you'd likely get
fired. You'd certainly be out of a job if you did it twice.

But today, we're not surprised to hear about mergers or
new projects or innovations that fail because of resistance
from white-collar workers. It seems like it's acceptable for an
executive or office worker to intentionally slow down innovation, to sabotage a merger, to sandbag a project that seems
threatening. Society accepts the reality that a knowledge worker

can misuse his time and effort, acting against a company's innovations.

We've embraced the upside of Henry Ford's bargain (getting paid a lot for work someone else could do), but since change has become the essential output of our work, we've abandoned our half of the deal. Idea workers get paid to change the rules. Many organizations are filled with people who are wrecking the punch press every day.

It's up to every manager—every employee, even—to call people on this behavior when we see it, and, if necessary, to take the punch press away.

> Your job is to make something happen.

So, Who's in Charge of Making Soft Innovations?

No one. That's the opportunity.

Almost every company I've researched and spoken with is organized the same way. Researchers research. Marketers market. Managers manage. Employees follow instructions. And nobody is in charge of soft innovation.

That's one big reason you see the neatest innovations coming from start-ups. Someone gets a great idea, can't find anyone who will implement it, and she's got no choice but to do it herself.

Of course, there are exceptions. There are companies with dynamic CEOs or, even better, dynamic middle managers who take responsibility for a constant stream of free prizes. Even though a few companies are smart enough to create these innovations, the vast majority of your competitors are sitting there doing the same-old-same-old, waiting to be picked off by you and your colleagues.

This is the safest bet I know in today's tumultuous business environment.

> The first one to create the right innovation succeeds.

Not All Great Ideas Come from the Top

While the articles on the covers of leading business magazines might imply that CEOs have all the big insights, Geoffrey Hunt, now senior VP at Osram Sylvania (the number-one seller of lightbulbs) proved otherwise. His innovation was to license the right to make Sylvania brand TVs and other consumer electronics to Funai, Proview and Brite Star. The hardest part was working the idea through the system. Working with General Counsel Jim Gass, who liked the idea of protecting the brand, Hunt sold the organization on having other organizations take over this huge segment of their market. Five years after selling in the idea, sales are running at $650 million a year, with growth indicating that they are closing in fast on $1 billion—that's far more than Sylvania ever sold when they were doing all the work.

Question One: Isn't This R&D's Job?

The research and development group is charged with creating innovations on a regular schedule, without disrupting the existing organization.

They're hamstrung. First, they have to make big bets, even though, by definition, big bets are hard to win and hard to time. Second, they have to use a top-down approach to figure out which ideas to pursue (which means senior people call the shots). And third, more often than not, the rest of the organization ignores them.

Xerox invented the Mac interface, yet gave it away after the folks at headquarters were unable to capitalize on it. IBM pioneered dozens of innovations—yet abandoned them after the organization couldn't figure out how to implement them.

In 2002, Microsoft spent more than $5 billion on R&D. What did they get for their money? Innovations like Bob, the talking paper clip, the lousy Entourage interface and the Xbox.

R&D is a bust. It's not because the people in the R&D department are bad. It's because the cards are stacked against them. Clayton Christensen demolished the idea that R&D is the solution in *The Innovator's Dilemma*, and it's actually much worse than you might imagine.

No organization ever created an innovation. People innovate, not companies.

The fact is, organizations must learn that there isn't a risk-free technique that always works. The minute we try to make innovation perfect, we cause it to disappear.

Organizations are paralyzed trying to figure out how to create top-down, risk-free bureaucracies that come up with breakthroughs, when the answer is quite the opposite.

Question Two: Then Where Does Soft Innovation Come From?

You.

If you decide that you want to make something great, more often than not your organization will follow you. And if they don't, there are a hundred organizations that will. I call the person who makes an innovation happen a champion. Without a champion, nothing happens.

Stop waiting. Stop whining. If you've got the desire to transform your job and your company, then there's absolutely nothing in your way. The rest of this book is dedicated to teaching you the techniques you need to do it right.

The perception of the way we should innovate is wrong. We've drawn it as a complicated, expensive process that should be done like most corporate initiatives: slowly, with massive buy-in and lots of planning.

Alas, the top-down approach doesn't work very well. Your CEO isn't very good at figuring out what to do next. Hiring teams of workers and squirreling them away in the R&D department doesn't work either.

Big-R&D-budget companies want to routinize inspiration and championship, but it doesn't work. Big pharmaceutical and technology companies are happy to spend billions on a process that attempts to produce breakthroughs on a regular schedule, and, by and large, they fail.

> Definition: "Champion" is a noun and a verb. A champion is someone in an organization who makes something happen. She takes a soft innovation and works the process until it reaches the marketplace.

Question Three: Do I Have to Do It Myself?

From the first day of school, they've been teaching you how to work in a factory. To sit in straight rows, talk in turn, follow instructions and do homework. Almost everything we do is modeled on repetitive factory work. Yet most knowledge workers change what they do every day. We don't work on the assembly line—now we work on projects.

Now, the highest leverage, the highest productivity, is in

groups that don't actually make anything—except they make things happen.

No one taught us how to do this, yet that's exactly what we have to do. Our productivity isn't in widgets per day. It's in innovations per hour.

No, you don't have to do this yourself. A project worth championing is a project worthy of a team. And understanding what it takes to collect, motivate and manage that team is a huge boost to your effort to get soft innovation done. The next section of this book shows you how to do just that.

The Gouliard Paradox: Why Things Don't Happen

Jay Gouliard is a brilliant marketer (he's currently VP of packaging development at General Mills). He's also good at talking about why companies get stuck.

"You can't introduce an innovative new package at the same cost that you've been running a highly optimized package for the last twenty years." Organizations like Jay's spend millions of dollars to wrest every last penny (and every last second) out of anything they manufacture. Companies resist change because, at least at first, the new stuff costs more (and appears to risk more) than the old stuff. Jay knows how big companies work. He knows that there's huge organizational resistance to free-prize thinking. The reason is simple: The status quo appears to be safer, cheaper and easier.

Gouliard works hard to create an environment that welcomes (and rewards) champions. He realizes that while it might cost more to introduce an innovation, the consumer is also willing to pay extra (sometimes a lot extra) for the free prize.

If General Mills continues to succeed against the bruising competition it faces throughout the supermarket, it's going to be because of Gouliard's culture shift. His competitors view change as a threat, something to throw lawyers at. He's building a team that views it as a requirement.

General Mills competes in twelve categories in the supermarket (from yogurt to my favorite food category, the oxymoron "frozen hot snacks"). In every single category, the company ranks either first or second in market share. When General Mills introduced Go-GURT (the yogurt that comes in a squeezable plastic LDPE tube), there's just no way their costs were comparable to a boring plastic or paper cup. But General Mills was smart enough to realize that people weren't just going to pay for the yogurt, they were paying for the fun (and convenience) of the package itself.

Years later, of course, the costs of this package are way down and they look smart. The difficult part was being brave at the beginning. They're doing it again with Nouriche, yogurt for grown-ups, which comes in a package that fits in your car's cup holder. As long as his competition is unwilling to challenge the status quo, unwilling to confront his paradox, then Jay wins.

Nobody Said It Was Easy

The thing about soft innovation and the creation of Purple Cows is that the very skills you are used to using to succeed aren't much help. Putting in a lot of hours, using up a lot of energy, staying away from home at all hours—that's painful and hard, but it's not what you need to do to be an innovator.

> Creating and championing free-prize projects isn't hard, but it is difficult.

Harry Truman made some difficult decisions. The most difficult, of course, was dropping the atomic bomb on Japan. The act itself wasn't hard for Truman—he signed a memo and it was done. Making the decision, taking the responsibility, living with the outcome—that was difficult.

Douglas MacArthur, on the other hand, managed a team that did hard work. He commanded hundreds of thousands of men and women, deployed millions of dollars in resources and performed an awesome task that was incredibly expensive.

I define difficult work as the stuff that takes guts or insight. It's not particularly dependent on how big your budget is or where you got a degree. Designing the profile for the Chrysler Building was difficult. Building it was hard.

Companies are pretty good at hard work. Hard work involves the management of projects and the deployment of assets. The people working on a project don't spend a lot of time worrying about whether it's ultimately going to be a success in the marketplace—instead, they worry about their role in the process.

Flying thousands of planes across the country every day is hard work. Publishing fifty thousand new books every year is hard work. Building millions of passenger cars every year is hard work.

Having the guts to change the timetable so that your planes aren't late, on the other hand, is difficult. So is publishing a book in a cereal box. And so is voluntarily launching an ultra-low-emissions automobile.

> Difficult work is easy to avoid. Difficult work is exactly what will get you promoted.

FIVE QUESTIONS

1. If our marketing were as good as it could be, would that be enough?

2. What are the innovations that are under my direct control?

3. Do we already offer consumers a free prize?

4. If we abandoned this product and created another, what would it be?

5. What are we afraid of?

SECTION 2
SELLING THE IDEA

I realize that most authors would talk about how to *make* the idea before they teach you how to *sell* it. That's backward. Knowing how to sell your idea—make it happen—is the step you must take before you bother inventing it. If you can't figure out how to implement your idea, there's no point in inventing it, is there? If you insist on reading section 3 first, it won't kill you, but I really wanted to hammer home the idea that you need to learn *how* to sell something before you focus on *what* to make.

Have You Ever Had a Great Idea?

It goes like this. You get to work, all excited about how you can launch, reinvent, galvanize, improve or remake some element of your company's product line. You start sharing the idea, maybe with your boss, or your co-workers, or Phil down in engineering.

Then it starts. Sometimes it's an eye roll. Sometimes it's "That's great, but . . ." And sometimes, if you've really stepped in it, you get the memo. The message is clear: "There are countless reasons this won't work. We've got a lot to do and we don't want to get sidetracked on some risky scheme. Sorry, but thanks for thinking outside the box!"

Your idea wasn't good enough. You're not sure why, but it's clear from the reaction that if your idea somehow had been better, the group would have embraced it. So it's back to the drawing board. Alas, for some people, after one too many episodes like this, you figure that you'll never have a good enough idea. So you give up.

Guess what?

> There's no correlation between how good your idea is and how likely the organization is to embrace it. None.

It's not about good ideas. It's about selling those ideas and making them happen.

It's All Marketing, Because the Product or the Service *Is* the Marketing

Marketing is no longer a separate division. It's the whole company.

Where marketing almost always fails is in the inability of the organization to actually do remarkable stuff. It's not because they don't know what to do, it's because they don't have champions to help them do it. So while this section might feel like it's about management, it's not. It's about marketing—because without managing the organization, marketing doesn't get done.

We Don't Need Your Innovation

"We have happy customers. We want to keep them happy."

People who are happy are your company's worst enemy.

Satisfied customers don't complain. Satisfied customers pay on time. Satisfied customers don't bother the boss or the tech support people or the legal department.

If the place where you work is successful at all, your company's biggest goal is probably to keep the satisfied customers happy.

This is a problem. It's a problem because satisfied customers are unlikely to radically increase your sales. Satisfied customers are unlikely to push you and your colleagues to stay ahead of the competition. One day, in fact, the competition will pass you and then the satisfied customers will quietly leave.

Your growth will come instead from the dissatisfied and the unsatisfied. The dissatisfied know that they want a solution, but aren't happy with the solution they've got. The minute they find it, they'll buy it. Yahoo!'s best customers weren't Google's first users. Nope. The happy Yahoo! customers weren't busy looking for a replacement. Google focused on dissatisfied Web surfers.

People who were online but weren't blown away by what they had been using (and *wanted* to be blown away).

The unsatisfied are the folks who don't even realize that they've got a problem that needs solving. That's why focus groups are often so useless. The people you really need to hear from are the great unwashed, the folks in the middle of the market who aren't even looking for you. That's where the real growth comes from, and where you will find the customers you need when your current product line becomes obsolete.

The problem is that management really *likes* those satisfied customers. The first question they'll ask about any innovation is, "Will our satisfied customers like it?" Of course, this is a silly question, because the satisfied customers already like what you've got. The question you ought to ask first is, "Will people dissatisfied with what they're using now embrace this, and, even better, will they tell the large number of unsatisfied people to go buy it right away?"

Southwest didn't sell to people who collected a ton of American Airlines frequent-flier miles. They sold to people who took the bus. Victoria's Secret didn't sell to people who were happy buying lingerie from the Frederick's of Hollywood catalog either. Instead, they created an entirely new market of consumers interested in buying nonsleazy sexy sleepwear.

I wore my Google T-shirt to the greenmarket in New York last week. No less than five people walked up to me and, without prompting, started a conversation about how much they loved Google. A tomato salesperson grabbed my arm, looked me right in the eye and said, "Google changed my life for the better. Google opened doors for me that I didn't know existed. Google is my friend. No [and then she raised her voice a few notches], Google is my *best friend*."

Now, if you've got satisfied customers like that, you're in trouble.

How do I know? I know because people used to say the same thing (well, close) to me when I wore my Yahoo! shirt to the greenmarket a few years ago. People loved Yahoo! to death. People loved the site and the stock so much that Yahoo! changed its focus from engaging the dissatisfied and the unsatisfied to trying to maintain its hold on the satisfied.

Go find some people who hate what you've got and who hate what your competitors have but still have a problem they want solved. Those are the folks who want the free prize.

How to Avoid Idea Failure

Almost all efforts at creating innovations within existing organizations fail. Why?

The reason is simple. Innovators are too focused on *what* the innovation is, not how they go about implementing it. Virtually every book on innovation focuses on exciting, sexy techniques like brainstorming, creativity and ideation.

The conceit is straightforward. You might think, "If I come

up with the correct answer, if I could somehow invent exactly what the market wants, then the organization will do the right thing and make it happen."

Alas, this doesn't match the reality of the situation.

I don't care how amazing your idea is. If you can't get it implemented, it's worthless.

Last year, Dyson sold more than $200 million worth of vacuum cleaners around the world. Theirs is a marvelous invention, fun to look at, a joy to use, and most important, possibly the very best vacuum cleaner ever invented. Even though it costs twice as much as a standard vacuum, it is the single best-selling vacuum in England (not only in sales, but units as well).

Yet James Dyson didn't set out to sell his own vacuum. He attempted to license the vacuum to every single vacuum cleaner marketer he could find. One by one, they rejected his idea.

Think about that for a second. Everyone—Electrolux, Hoover, Miele—had the chance to embrace the idea, to license it and dominate the market. All of them refused.

No one argues *now* that Dyson didn't have a great idea. For years, though, that great idea was inches away from never being built, and the companies that turned him down were quick to point out that they were being entirely rational in declining to market it—the idea wasn't good enough, apparently. Were they right? Was it that Dyson didn't have a good enough idea? Of course not. A quick look at all the Dyson knockoff vacuum cleaners on the market today is proof that his idea was terrific.

Turning No into Yes

The reason for focus groups, market research and the like is the continuing mirage that somehow, if we do enough work, we can figure out in advance if we have the right idea or not. After all, organizations believe that if they know what the right idea is, they'll do it. But if our resistance to ideas has nothing to do with the ideas themselves and everything to do with the process, it's clear that all of these steps are merely designed to assuage our fear or create yet another hurdle for the innovator.

No organization innovates. People innovate. And the innovations that actually get produced are the ones with a successful champion behind them.

Champions turn no into yes. Champions understand that the internal sales process is at least as important as the idea itself. Champions are able to bring together all of the elements they need to turn a soft innovation into a free prize, creating a Purple Cow that reaches the market and, more likely than not, transforms an industry.

People who are good at championing succeed more often than people who are good at inventing. I'm challenging you to focus on the difficult part (championing) and we'll get to the fun part (inventing) later!

The Cart and the Horse

Starting with the innovation and then figuring out how to sell it is the main reason innovations fail. We pick something too big or too small or launch the project the wrong way and—*boom*—it's dead.

Salespeople understand this. A great salesperson won't join a company if she believes the method of selling doesn't match the product itself. First you figure out the who and the how of the selling, *then* you figure out the product.

So, this section of the book is designed to teach you how to champion an innovation. Then, in the last section, we'll figure how to build something you can champion successfully.

Becoming a Champion

It's up to you.

That's a simple statement, but it's so different from the way most people approach the innovation process. Remember the $5-a-day man at Ford? Well, his job was to take a piece of metal and punch a hole in it. That was way more productive than farming, and he got paid a lot to do it. What he did wasn't up to him. What he did was based on the instructions he got from his boss. Period.

Your job is *not* to do the same thing over and over again. Your job is to create productivity by inventing a new fashion.

You have the time.

You have the skill.

If you accept that it's up to you, you can jump-start your career and turbocharge your company, too. That's the first step—accepting the responsibility.

I Dare You to Do Something Great

Some people may believe that they don't have the talent, the skill or the guts to create and implement the innovations that go into a free prize. This is silly. Of course you do.

As you'll see, the one thing that every successful innovator has in common is the will to get things done. If you want to succeed, you probably will.

The techniques I describe in the rest of this book are designed to channel your will and effort into a project worthy of your time. You need to start by believing that you can make a difference, that you can contribute to the project. Once you've made that decision (and no one can tell you otherwise!) the rest of the tactics are straightforward.

There are only two reasons to hesitate: Either you don't know how to get your organization to implement what you create (that's what this section will teach you) or you don't think you have any ideas worth building (that's what the next section covers). Neither is impossible, it just takes energy.

> Go ahead, do something great.
>
>   Champion a soft innovation.
>
>   I dare you.

No Cow Gets Sold Without a Champion

Take a look at every Purple Cow, every remarkable product, every free prize, and sooner or later, you'll find a champion.

The status quo doesn't need defending—but your idea does.

Sooner or later, every project runs into trouble. Usually, it's because people within the organization encounter insurmountable obstacles. Of course, they're not really insurmountable, they're just difficult. Without a champion navigating through these obstacles, most projects will slow down and eventually stop. Someone who cares too little won't put in the effort to overcome the obstacles, they'll give up and walk away.

Worse than stopping, though, is the second barrier to creating a free prize: The forces of mediocrity will band together to water down your innovation. They'll try to make it more popular, easier to understand, easier to build, easier to fit within the existing retail/factory/media business model. Well-meaning folks will water down your edgy idea into something safer, without realizing that their contribution makes the idea riskier.

The Choice Is Between Following the Rules or Doing the Right Thing

Everyone's got great ideas. If you don't have enough ideas, the next section will show you a reliable way to find more. The difference between success and failure most definitely is not about any shortage of ideas that are good enough. Instead, it's about overcoming the status quo and inertia and working within your organization to make things happen.

The good news is that this is exactly what your boss wants you to do, it's fun, it's rewarding and once you learn how to do it, you're guaranteed a good job for the rest of your life. The bad news is that it's difficult and sometimes lonely.

Whoever you wish to be—a champion or someone who lets everyone else worry about a project—you have to make a choice, a conscious decision to be that person. By embracing this choice, by announcing it (to yourself and, ultimately, to others), you make the process far more likely to succeed.

All Industries Are Not the Same

It sure helps to sell what people are buying. That sounds obvious, but it's easy to miss. In the book business, publishers buy fifty thousand new book ideas every year. Most of them are boring run-of-the-mill releases. But there's always a hunt going on, there's always a desire to find the next soft innovation and bring it to market, to create a free prize. The toy industry buys thousands of ideas a year for precisely the same reason. The tool industry, on the other hand, is afraid of innovation. Most companies in this industry want nothing to do with a free prize.

If your temperament for invention and fashion doesn't match your market, it doesn't matter how good a champion you are—it's going to be a long and lonely road! I recently had a meeting with a friend of a friend. For years, Ken has been working to create a major fashion overhaul for hand tools. Imagine saws and hammers and pliers that worked better, looked better and were more fun to buy.

Ken has built prototypes. He has great collateral materials. And he's been thrown out of most of the major tool manufacturers' offices. The reason is that tool manufacturers are not ready to buy what he has to sell. All of them want to follow the leader, and none of them want to *be* the leader.

Ken's challenge is to find a partner who wants to lead the giants in the direction they need to go. He doesn't have the leverage to do it in a meeting or with a proposal. So if he cares enough, his best plan is to go it alone and teach them a lesson in the marketplace. (Actually, a better plan is to not bother inventing a better hand tool when you could easily invent something just as cool for a more receptive industry—any farmer will tell you that fertile land is much more important than better seeds.) The mismatch between great ideas and stuck industries explains why so many earth-shattering free prizes come from entrepreneurs. If the industry isn't buying your idea, you must either walk away or champion it yourself from outside.

Can You Do It Alone?

If you can, you probably should. It's not unheard-of to create a free prize on your own. If you're a real-estate agent, an artist or a landscape architect, you can probably do something to your business or your work that is truly remarkable.

The rest of us, though, have to count on others. We need organizations filled with people, money and other assets to help realize our dreams. We need their leverage.

In order to make a lever work, of course, you need a fulcrum.

Introducing the Fulcrum of Innovation

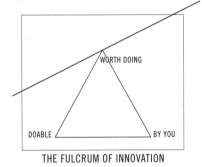

THE FULCRUM OF INNOVATION

We start by recognizing that selling an organization on an idea is a process, a specific set of steps that probably shouldn't be done on an ad hoc basis. If you walk in on Monday morning and start blurting out your brand new idea to everyone you meet, it's unlikely that you'll have much of a project left by the end of the day.

In order to get leverage from your organization, you'll need their willing help. And that only comes if you've got a fulcrum— a leverage point that magnifies your efforts and your ideas and turns them into reality. Too often, people with big ideas forget to invest in finding and reinforcing the fulcrum that will give them the leverage they need to actually get something done.

It turns out that building that fulcrum—I call it the fulcrum of innovation—is a challenge that is the same across almost every organization. The successes all look alike. Regardless of what you do and who you do it with, the steps to build your fulcrum (and get the leverage you need) remain the same.

The fulcrum of innovation is the result of the surprisingly small set of questions that people will ask themselves as they consider your idea. They are:

* Is it going to be successful?

* Is it worth doing?

* Is this person able to champion the project?

If the answer to any of these questions is a resounding no, it's unlikely your project will happen. Understanding how the three pieces fit together and what to do about them is a big part of choosing the right project and getting it done. Build a strong enough fulcrum and the leverage you will exert will exceed everyone's expectations.

Remember, these people don't care a bit about what *your* answer to these three questions might be. What matters is what *they* think the answer is, based on the evidence you give them.

IS IT GOING TO BE SUCCESSFUL?

This sounds obvious, but the thing is, most people like to work on projects that are going to succeed. The stupid thing is that there's no way in the world to know if they are going to be successful in advance! More often than not, a Purple Cow is a surprise hit, not a sure thing. The act of trying to guarantee the success of an innovation is almost certain to make it *less likely* that it will succeed.

So, here's another paradox. In order for the fulcrum to work, you've got to persuade people you've got something that's a sure thing. But the more certain it appears, the less likely it really is to succeed.

Later on, I'll tell you about skeumorphs—techniques you can use to make your revolutionary new idea seem safer and more traditional. The important point here is that if you act as though it's a sure thing, if you present it with confidence and as more than a wild notion, you're far more likely to get the support you need.

IS IT WORTH DOING?

Even if it's likely to succeed, it's still going to be a lot of work. There's time, there's risk and there's the personal effort necessary to take something from nowhere to a shipping product.

This means that you've got to figure out what each person you're selling to thinks is important. Some of your co-workers think a project is worth doing if it's a cool challenge. Others will be attracted to an idea that's going to make the stock price go up. Still others might be sold on your idea if they believe it will make their jobs more secure, or make the world a better place, or get their picture in the newspaper or make a currently horrible part of their job less horrible.

Figuring out who wants what—and then playing that back to them—is an essential part of using the fulcrum properly.

IS THIS PERSON ABLE TO CHAMPION THE PROJECT?

This is the one question that probably hasn't occurred to you. If you're one of those people who complain, "I have all these great ideas, but my boss won't let me do anything!" then this question describes your real problem.

I've met quite a few bosses, and I can count on one hand the number who don't want an employee to shepherd a project that is likely to succeed, worth doing *and* well within the capabilities of the person who wants to do it.

In fact, it's your boss's dream for you to do this.

If you've been getting turned down again and again, it's almost certainly because your vision of the fulcrum doesn't match the organization's vision. You've been fooling yourself, believing that your audience has more confidence in the three corners of your fulcrum than they actually do.

Most likely, they don't think you can handle it . . . because your audacity doesn't match your reputation for execution. It's not that you don't have great ideas—you do. The problem lies in their scale and in your role as champion. That's why Steven Spielberg has an easier time making a movie than you do—his backers know he can make it happen.

Some people get lucky. At exactly the right moment in their career, the boss plucks them from obscurity, gives them the royal imprimatur and puts them in charge. This works great for you because it automatically makes you the champion and encourages everyone to do what you say.

Alas, this almost never happens. It almost never happens because your boss doesn't know when you're ready. She doesn't know that you want to do it. And most of all, she's so busy running the company it never occurred to her to build something truly remarkable along the way.

You can keep waiting to get plucked from obscurity, or you can learn how to champion your project one person at a time.

The Fulcrum Drives Your Choice of Strategy

If you've got a great reputation, a lot of personal power within the organization, a wonderful idea for a project that's sure to succeed and the solution to a burning problem within the organization, it may be appropriate to use a top-down strategy. Get a meeting with your boss, sell her on the idea and then take it, with her stamp of approval, to the highest-level person you can find.

This top-down approach cuts through a great deal of resource allocation trouble. It gives you the power to run your own show with the assets you need to get your project done. You'll still have all sorts of challenges along the way, but your course will be clearly laid out.

This is the fastest, easiest strategy, and, as you've probably guessed, it doesn't happen very often.

On the other hand, if you're working your way up the ladder, you've got a lot more flexibility in the way the project is handled, and you won't face a go/no-go decision so early. You can spend a lot of informal time with co-workers and evolve prototypes until the project has enough momentum that the higher-ups see a well-formed fulcrum and give you their blessings. This is the way it usually works. You work with passionate peers to build a fulcrum that's strong enough on all three points to make your bosses look smart for giving you the go-ahead.

ARE YOU THE GUY?

If your posture at work has been to do what you're told, it's going to be difficult to persuade people that you're ready to champion a major new innovation. Instead, you've got to start early
and start small. Start with lunch.

Lunch needs a champion. Lunch involves picking a place,
persuading everyone that you picked the right place, collecting
(or better yet, delegating) the orders, dispatching someone to
pick it up, splitting up the change, making sure the wrappers get
thrown out.

Lots of people know how to champion lunch, of course. But
most stop there. Big mistake.

After you champion lunch, start championing customer service issues, or divisive (but trivial) items like the new company
logo. As each project comes and goes, you'll develop essential
skills, and, just as important, demonstrate to your organization
that you can handle it.

I don't mean that you need to become an expert—champions
rarely are. You don't need to make yourself out to be the person
who knows all the answers. What you must do, though, is know
the questions.

I was in a meeting the other day with five people. Two of us
were fairly senior. One, Allison, was obviously the most junior. I
could tell that she had decided before the meeting started not to
say anything. Through my interactions with her, though, I knew

how smart she was. So when the meeting reached an impasse, I asked her for her opinion.

She hesitated for a second, then asked a question that completely changed the tone of the meeting and the outcome of the discussion we were having. She blew the meeting wide open.

What if Allison had made a different choice than the one she had made before the meeting? If she made a commitment to herself to actively participate in every meeting and to volunteer to run any task force at every opportunity, she'd accomplish two things: First, her work would get more interesting. Second, she'd be grooming herself to be seen as qualified to handle a big challenge when the next opportunity came along.

> It's hard to imagine a better way to ensure job security.

IS IT WORTH DOING?

To a man about to drown, even a brick is a potential life raft. The trick is persuading your peers that without an innovation, you're all in trouble. Your idea is better than a brick, of course, which makes your desperate colleagues delighted to grab ahold.

Sooner or later, every company gets sold or folds. Nothing lasts forever, especially organizations. Why do they disappear with such regularity? More often than not, it's because they believe that they are immortal, destined for eternal success, in no need of help of any kind. Your organization needs your help to see that (without your idea) trouble looms ahead.

Many companies (or charities, or governments) that fail are so confident in their top-dog status they make it a habit to reject potential free prizes as not worth their time and energy. They are still comfortable with the momentum from their last Purple Cow, and it's always easier to coast than to reinvent.

My local (but now bankrupt) Italian place, Manzi's Restaurant, decided it didn't need to update the menu. Hoover decided they didn't need the Dyson vacuum cleaner. Gray Davis decided he could ignore the rising outcry in California. It goes on and on.

Before you try to sell the organization on why your new innovation is worth doing, you need to invest time denigrating the status quo. Once people understand how the current situation can't help but decay, and ultimately fail, they're far more likely to listen to your new idea.

The status quo almost always looks rosy because people are naturally optimistic. They assume that things will stay the way they are. But we all know that nothing lasts forever, and if you can identify your organization's weaknesses, you can lay the groundwork for your free prize.

Let's say you've got a great idea about revamping your company's approach to customer service. If 12 percent of all customer service calls currently end without a successful resolution, grab that statistic. Then build on it. Describe how each of these calls leads to negative word of mouth, which spreads. Share stories of how this negative ideavirus has affected your brand.

If possible, find specific examples of customers who have defected. Tell stories of how the hard work of the sales force, factory crew and marketing people has been undone because of these incidents. Assemble photos, letters and case studies.

Whenever you're asked to talk about your idea, start by going through the litany of what's currently broken. Be specific, not general. Give the crisis a face and fill in the details.

Is this fair? Of course not. But do you think for a moment that your opponents will hesitate for a second to describe the imaginary problems your new idea might cause? Of course not.

By focusing on what's broken now, you lower the bar. You create a sense of urgency. You make it really clear that *action must be taken*.

> When they must do *something*, and you are the best available champion, it'll get done.

IS IT GOING TO WORK?

If you're working on a truly remarkable idea, then, by definition, there's no way in the world you can prove it's going to work.

Gary Hamel likes to talk about how absurd the meetings at Gillette must have been when they launched the Mach III razor.

"I know," one guy says, "we did a one-blade razor, then a two-blade . . . [puzzled looks, waiting to see where he's taking this crazy idea] how about a three-blade razor!" Even with this crushing logic in their favor, Gillette spent millions on test marketing and focus groups to prove to themselves that their idea was certain to work.

Of course, your idea isn't as obvious as the Mach III. If you've got to prove that Hotmail or the Yomega yo-yo or the fuzzy logic rice cooker is going to be a hit, you've got quite a row to hoe.

I think the answer lies in skeumorphs. This involves hiding the truly remarkable elements of your free prize behind comfortable features that people can believe in. Even though the watch on your wrist is digitally controlled, it still has hands. Postage meters still use symbols that look a hundred years old. Toyota's new Prius still looks like a car.

There's a bar in New York called Vynl (it's way too hip for me, so I've never been inside). They have a very cool sign out front. The sign is remarkable, but the hardware holding it to the building is not. The brackets and screws are exactly what you'd expect them to be. They didn't have to reinvent the very idea of a sign in order to put up something cool.

Do you have to insist that focus groups are ridiculous and refuse to do them? Not at all. If a focus group is what it's going to take to get this part of the fulcrum to work, do it! Just be sure you're running the group for the correct reason (to get people to say they love your idea), not to get actual feedback (because, of course, they have no clue).

The goal in building this part of the fulcrum is not to prove beyond any doubt that your idea will work. That's impossible. The goal is to go through the steps necessary for your colleagues to *believe* (because they want to believe) that it will work. It's an emotional ticket you need stamped, not an intellectual one.

> Anchor your remarkable innovation firmly in a proven, tested foundation.

The Reason the Fulcrum Matters

It's so tempting to gloss over the fulcrum and jump right into the good stuff—coming up with the next great idea. After all, our instincts tell us, it's the idea that matters. If we know what to do, it'll happen.

As we've seen, though, every innovation must first gather a team to make it happen. It must jump through a thousand hoops before it reaches the marketplace. And for every innovation that *hasn't* made it, the reason is the same: Something was wrong with the fulcrum. Until you understand the hurdles you're going to have to overcome, don't bother trying to invent the next great product.

Organizations don't fail because they don't have any good ideas. Organizations fail because they don't have champions who understand how to use the fulcrum.

> An idea is just an idea until it gets leveraged by an organization and embraced by the market.

Summarizing the Fulcrum

Since selling your idea is a process, you approach the three points of the fulcrum in a step-by-step manner from the very first day.

* Build your reputation as a champion in advance.

* Denigrate the status quo before you present anything.

* Find the handles that your audience needs to give them security to believe in the idea.

Remember, your organization's adoption of your idea is going to have nothing whatsoever to do with whether it's a good idea or not. These are the three gates through which you must pass in order to proceed.

My Yahoo! Story

One of the very best ideas I ever had is immortalized in patent #00972262.0-2212-US0028816 (EEU).

Soon after arriving at Yahoo! in 1999, I combined a number of unrelated ideas into a plan that would have ensured Yahoo!'s domination of the Web for all time. In a nutshell, the idea was to give Yahoo! users (there were more than a hundred million registered at that time) "frequent-surfer points" for clicking where we asked them to.

Obviously, creating an attention currency would be incredibly valuable. Giving people points to click on a banner or respond to an e-mail or choose one search result over another would have a dramatic impact on influencing the click stream. It would also keep people from switching to another service. The next step would be to allow this currency to go Webwide, giving other sites the ability to buy points from Yahoo! (the way other companies buy miles from American Airlines). Everyone from Amazon to bloggers would be buying and selling these points, with Yahoo! acting as a middleman. Yahoo! could create an attention economy, and my boss would be Alan Greenspan.

The real home run was the way we planned to have people cash in the points. Obviously, we couldn't afford to give prizes to each and every user merely for clicking. Even in the dot-com days, that would be foolish. Instead, I devised a plan where people could enter a monthly auction and *bid* (with points) for the millions of dollars worth of prizes we'd assemble. This way, even though the number of points would get higher and higher, the number of prizes would be stable. We'd fund the prizes with the money the other sites paid us for their points and for their ads.

Not only was this program going to ensure our longtime domination, it was going to make a profit. It was eBay meets frequent-flier miles.

So what happened? Was something wrong with my idea?

I didn't know a thing about the fulcrum. I did know, deep down, that this idea would work. We had the market power, the technology was not difficult, and users would respond. It was a $100-million-a-year business without blinking.

I also believed that it would be worth doing. Ensuing events have proven me right—that Yahoo! was not unassailable in search, and by making a sticky currency, Yahoo! could make a small investment in long-term success.

So I met with my boss and his team, laid out the idea and waited for everyone to get excited and then go build it. I figured it wasn't my job to build and market this, and I assumed that the organization would coalesce around my terrific idea and roll it out.

It was a total failure.

My new boss didn't believe I was the right person to champion this project. He didn't know me or trust me, and I didn't have roots in the organization. Everyone else was up to their eyeballs in work, so even though people thought it was great, no one else in the room was willing to volunteer to champion my idea. Worse, I so believed in the idea that I didn't think it was necessary to challenge the status quo, to outline why this project was worth doing. "These are smart guys," I thought. "If they want to pursue this idea, they will."

It sat there, collecting mildew, and finally disappeared. The fulcrum won. It always does.

The tragedy of my arrogance was that if I had known what I was doing, I would have taken a very different approach. The first step would have involved volunteering to champion someone else's project, something that could be executed pretty quickly. With that person's support (people never forget when you champion something for them), I would have established roots in the organization and built the connections needed to be the champion for one of my own ideas, albeit a smaller one. After successfully championing a few projects, it would have been far easier to successfully pitch the world-changing Web points idea.

It's so easy to say, "My boss won't let me." It's even easier to say, "I don't have a good enough idea." Most of the time, neither one is really what's stopping you. You're stopped because you don't have leverage. And you don't have leverage because you didn't build the fulcrum properly.

Who Decides?

Almost every organization has small pockets of power. These are made up of those extremely influential individuals who have an opinion that's worth more than the average person's. You need to figure out who these influencers are, who they listen to and what they want.

Getting the fulcrum right doesn't help if you're doing it with the wrong people. A major company I'm familiar with had a huge split between two levels in the organization. The people at the top wanted to do innovative, groundbreaking projects. They wanted to find the free prizes that would build the Purple Cows that would continue, and even accelerate, their growth.

At the next level were four senior managers who had fallen prey to Henry Ford's paradox. They were making a fortune in stock options, and desperately did not want to screw up. These four gatekeepers made sure that nothing unpredictable ever got past them and up to the most senior managers. As a result, the company went into an entirely predictable tailspin, with smaller competitors stealing market share courtesy of the mediocrity these four were embracing.

It was seductive for any champion to go to the welcoming middle managers and present an idea. The idea, of course, would be described by the innovator in a way that mimicked the very public pronouncements of senior management. This is exciting! This is what we're here for!

The ideas were killed. The would-be champions had fallen into a trap. They confused the excellent listening skills of middle management with genuine enthusiasm for change. These guys wanted predictability, not excitement.

So why not go to the top? Because the executives at the top were smart enough to know that if they ignored their four middle managers, they'd lose their support while being deluged with harebrained schemes.

Far better, it turns out, would be to go to the four managers with a much more balanced presentation. Not focused solely on the worth of the new idea, but balanced with a discussion of the current state of the market. Point out how the status quo is about to crack, fail, die, wither or otherwise embarrass the organization (not a lot of stability in that!). Make it clear that the stock options are in jeopardy. Describe the emergency. Provide *proof* that the new idea is more certain, more reliable and easier to guarantee than what's happening now. Make it easy to believe.

The ideas that got accepted were important ideas wrapped in a uniform that middle management could embrace. By focusing on how these innovations would bring more stability, ensure the status quo and reduce risk, the champions were able to get past these gatekeepers and make it to market.

> What matters to you doesn't matter.
>
> What matters to the organization matters.

A Passel of Tactics

The rest of this section is devoted to a grab bag of tactics that will work some of the time for some of the champions.

Tactic: Ask Questions

My first real job involved informally managing forty world-class software engineers in a bet-the-company launch of five major new software products. This would have been a great opportunity, but I had almost failed out of my computer classes in college, and all I knew how to do was replace the toner cartridge in the printer.

Which turned out to be a major asset.

Everyone knew that I couldn't possibly have a point of view when it came to engineering issues, so they were happy to have me kibitz. I spent my entire day going from one team to another, asking questions.

Please don't think that you've got to know all the answers, that you must have the entire plan laid out. You don't. You just need the posture of a champion and the guts to ask hard questions.

Tactic: Ask Obligating Questions

Every free prize needs a champion because organizations don't like change. People will put roadblocks in your way. They'll object. They'll explain why it can't be done.

Generally, it's a bad idea to answer objections. If you spend all your time answering one objection after another, sooner or later the people you're selling to will find an objection you can't answer. Better to answer an objection with a question.

When someone says, "We'll never be able to put the book in a box because then we'll need two ISBN numbers," start by understanding the objection. "What's the problem with two ISBN numbers?" is a good way to start. Keep working your way backward until you uncover the actual problem—not the symptom of the problem.

Then, before you try to answer the objection associated with the real problem, take two more shots. First, ask, "If we can solve this problem, can you see any other reason not to move ahead?" This obligates the person to speak up or put up. It means that the objection you're going to tackle is the real problem, not a stalling tactic. Second, work to get them on your side. Ask, "If I could persuade you that solving this problem was really important, how would you do it?"

Tactic: Let Them Pee on Your Idea

When you present your vision of a free prize, some people within your organization are looking for certainty, for a lead to follow, for a complete vision. Others, often those in positions to hurt (or help) your cause, want to pee on your idea as a way of marking their territory.

Let them.

The minute an executive changes your idea in a harmless way, it becomes his idea. And now that it's *his* idea, you both win. Some champions go so far as to intentionally overlook details in their concepts, to make it easier for someone in power to dramatically improve their idea. Why not?

Tactic: Think Like an Artist

I was lucky enough to come across a book by David Bayles and Ted Orland called *Art and Fear*. They wrote this magnificent (and short) book for artists, but I realized that the same challenges an artist faces are faced by innovators as well. Here's what every champion must remember:

1. DON'T QUIT

Stopping is different from quitting. If you are ahead of your time, or the organizational dynamic is stacked against you, you can stop (for a while). You can switch tracks. You can stop often. But real artists (and real champions) don't quit.

2. THE CHALLENGE IS NOT COMING UP WITH A GREAT IDEA, BUT HOLDING ON TO IT

First, stop keeping your ideas a secret. Ideas in secret die. They need light and air or they starve to death. The more people you share your idea with, the more likely it is to become real.

A second lesson is even more important—it's not the idea that matters, it's what you do with it. The real challenge (and the real skill) comes from championing your idea, shepherding it through the system and turning it into a reality.

Even though ideas themselves are worthless, you must protect their purity. At every step along the way, people will try to corrupt your idea. Your job as a champion is to say no. Embrace the essence of the idea and maintain that essence as the idea goes from your head to the marketplace.

Yes, there are an infinite number of ideas that are good enough. But once you choose one, it becomes *your* idea and you have to defend it from becoming average.

3. AVOID THE MYTH OF THE PERFECT

As we've seen, if they don't like your idea, it's not necessarily the idea that's the problem. Stop trying to be perfect and realize that doing the best you can might be enough. There are no silver bullets, no innovations that are certain to galvanize the marketplace and solve all problems.

4. NO HOME RUNS, NO SHORTCUTS

Every struggling artist dreams of lunch with Phillipe De Montebello, director of the Metropolitan Museum of Art. Every Web entrepreneur imagines a feature on the home page of Google.

Shortcuts are the things of legend. Bruce Springsteen got a shortcut to fame when he showed up simultaneously on the cover of *Time* and *Newsweek* after his third album came out. *American Idol* is about nothing but shortcuts.

Your idea, alas, won't benefit from the same treatment. It will take longer than you anticipate and work less powerfully than you hope. But that's okay, because it's the process that matters. Once you master the process, it keeps getting easier.

If you don't bet on the home run, you'll be happy with the singles and doubles. If you don't focus all your energy on the one breakthrough bet, you are more likely to succeed, aren't you?

5. PEOPLE DON'T LIKE TO SAY NO

When Nathan Michaud, program officer for community planning and development at the Island Institute, hatched his plan to track lobsters by using imprinted rubber bands, no one in his organization said no. Of course, no one said, "Yes, do it!" either. There are plenty of organizations where the usual response is to do nothing, or to stall, or to object, but not too strenuously. A project with a champion will prevail in each of these cases.

If you can look someone in the eye and say, "I'm going to make this happen unless you insist that I stop," more often than not, you'll get what you ask for.

All five of these principles are here to sell you on committing to a process. Understanding that leveraging your idea through an organization is a journey, not an event, can dramatically increase the chances that you're actually going to succeed. The most successful champions stand up and say, "This is the journey.

We are going to be formal about it and we're going to do it purposefully. These are the steps . . ."

Part of holding on to your idea is knowing when to say no. Does that mean you need to be bullheaded? Of course not. One of the fine lines in championing a project is understanding when feedback makes it better and when feedback makes it mediocre. Steve Jobs fought for years when smart people told him that early versions of the Mac needed to have an accessible case and an easy way for people to add memory cards and such. He (foolishly) argued with them, insisting on the purity of his vision. (The battle got so heated that Apple executive Jean Louis Gasee had license plates that read OPENMAC.) The mistake Jobs made was not realizing that allowing people to customize their Macs would not damage his core vision, but would have opened up significant new markets.

Compare this decision to Jeff Hawkin's decision not to add a bunch of features to the Palm the first few years it was on the market. The entire appeal of the device was that it wasn't jammed with confusing stuff—by insisting on keeping his idea pure, he allowed it to spread.

Henry Ford could have had the best of both worlds. The reason he only made Model T cars in black was that you could paint a car black in less than half the time. Other colors took too long. Slowing down the painting process would have raised the price too high, damaging his initial vision.

The mistake he made was not creating an alternative, higher-priced model until after the competition made huge headway. The Model T was the car that taught people that once they had enough money, they should buy a more expensive car from the competition. Ford could have been the competition, too.

Tactic: Sell Individuals, Not the Organization

Calling a big meeting is almost never a good idea. Big meetings are terrific for setting milestones or dictating your thoughts to a willing audience. But big meetings are absolutely terrible for introducing a new idea.

* Everyone wants to know what the others think.

* Everyone wants to be in the loop, the earlier the better.

You can take advantage of both needs by having informal conversations with individuals. Focus on the part that *they* need to hear, and honestly tell them it's the first time you're discussing the particular element. In the words of Rich Gioscia, now head of design at Palm, "you don't convince people in a team meeting. You work the channels."

When Steve Gundrum introduced dinosaur-shaped pasta to Chef Boyardee, he got the money he needed to pay for his focus groups by going to the advertising department. He explained to them that if the rest of the company got behind his idea, there'd be a lot more money to spend on ads to launch it! If he'd called a big meeting, groupthink would have stamped out his silly idea. But by courting people one faction at a time, he made it work.

Tactic: Dare Them to Improve Your Idea

Get them on your side of the table, doodling on the same pad, working as co-conspirators. Instead of focusing on how the idea represents a threat to their domain, focus on how it can help fix the problems in the other departments!

As you first start interacting with people about your idea, you should keep two goals in mind:

1. Encourage each person to make your idea better.

2. Get each person you meet with to start thinking of it as his idea.

Even people who are afraid of change and in love with the status quo have big enough egos to indulge in brainstorming with you about improving what you're working on. They're especially interested in doing that if your idea will help them fix what they see as a problem. Get them in deep enough and you've created an ally.

Tactic: Acknowledge the Status Quo
(and What's Wrong with It)

If your idea is designed to augment or replace the status quo, you better make it crystal clear how much trouble the existing state of affairs is going to cost your company if you don't take action *now*. No one wants to be the voice of doom. But better to be a naysayer before it's too late.

While it's easy to shy away from this approach, it's extraordinarily important. By saying it out loud, you engage in a conversation that makes it clear to both sides what's at stake. You should do this *before* you tell people your idea. The reason that almost all the online music ventures failed was that eager entrepreneurs assumed that the record industry understood how much trouble it was about to be in.

It wasn't until Apple came along that things aligned. Why? The biggest reason is that Apple waited until the pain was truly significant. They then applied all three parts of the fulcrum perfectly. In its first month, Apple generated more online music revenue than all previous ventures over the last decade, combined.

Tactic: Build a Prototype

The astonishing thing is not how easy it is to make a prototype. You can make a prototype of any Web site in Photoshop. You can visually prototype virtually any product using a Mac. And now you can actually make cheap physical prototypes of objects using extruded plastic "printers." Need a prototype of a user interface or a voice mail system? It's all trivial.

What's astonishing is how infrequently people actually use them!

The first time you see Reebok Travel Trainers or the Segway or the iPod or the new Nokia music phone, you get it. But until you hold it in your hands, it's merely a concept, a flaky idea, something that might (or might not) happen.

A prototype makes an idea concrete. It makes not one, but all three elements of the fulcrum more real. To hold it makes it possible, it makes it likely and it reinforces your role as the champion, the owner of the vision.

Prototypes also help us get over our desire to make it perfect before we start. If it's easy to make one prototype, it's easy to make a hundred. Each prototype gets better, more useful, more real.

Walk into a meeting with a key power broker. Announce you've got a prototype in your briefcase. That's all she wants to see. Now you've got her. Take your time. Denigrate the status quo. Lay out the vision. *Now,* let her hold the prototype. Put it on her desk. *Leave* it on her desk!

As the days go by, people will pass the desk, see the prototype and ask about it. As each person gets more and more excited about this cool innovation, the word spreads. It becomes a reality. All that's left is to actually make it.

Paul Sagel is the inventor of the Crest Whitestrips, one of the most successful new product launches at Procter & Gamble in many years. The key moment in selling this radical soft innovation to a very large bureaucracy came when he pitched it to senior management.

He did two things. First, he brought in the parts for his prototype and built it right there, on the spot, to show how easy it
was. Second, and far cooler, a few days before the meeting, he
had his teeth whitened. They glowed. Paul, it turns out, *was* the
prototype.

Tactic: The Gimme Cap

Once your idea starts spreading through the organization, there
will be only two teams: for you, and against you.

If you're doing your job as a champion, more and more people will start to realize how they will benefit from the innovation you're rolling out. You need to make it easy for them to let
the rest of the group know that they share your vision. So give
them a cap. Or a T-shirt. Any easily visible way to let the world
know they're on board.

By making their agreement visible, you spread the word. You
also increase the perception that the project is going to happen,
that it is more likely to succeed, that it is worth doing, and most
of all, since you're the guy who got all these individuals involved, that you're the person to run it.

People often say they'll know it when they see it. They won't.
These are the same people who didn't buy Microsoft stock at
the IPO, didn't buy real estate in Telluride and didn't think *The
Lord of the Rings* would be a successful movie. Don't believe that
everyone will be fair and rational. It's not true. They won't be.
These people care most of all about other people's opinion of

your idea, not the idea itself! You win by building constituencies that are afraid of the alternative to supporting your idea.

One of the best ways to change the mind of the group is to have the group see tangible proof that everyone else is changing their mind as well.

> Groupthink is bad, except when it's helping!

Keith Yamashita created a really neat device. He printed hundreds of black-and-white buttons that said STUCK. Then he printed the same number of buttons (but smaller) that said UN. In his work as a designer and agent of change, Keith is constantly faced with overcoming inertia and skepticism. The two-button approach works wonders. Obviously, the people against whatever he was trying to roll out could have worn the STUCK button, but probably didn't. Those on board could wear *both* buttons. It spread. It gave Keith the momentum he needed to get people over the hump.

Tactic: Invent a Vocabulary

What do you call a bottle of Pepsi that a teenager can drink in less than six seconds?

At a company where maximizing consumption among teens is a primary goal, having a word for this attribute is essential. They actually have *two* words: "slam" and "gulpability."

Now that you've got words, it's easier to have a conversation about what you're trying to accomplish, isn't it? A brand manager can pitch a two-liter plastic bottle to management using a simple sentence, "It'll work because it doubles gulpability."

Ultimately, championing an idea through your organization is about persuading people to see the world through a different lens. And one of the best ways to do that is to give them new things to measure, new words for complicated concepts.

Apple doesn't talk about its products with the same words that Dell uses. Apple talks about user experience and sexiness. Dell talks about speed and cost. The products they create reflect the words they use.

Tactic: Take a Little

Bill Winkelman invented the Starbucks Card, which now accounts for an astonishing 10 percent of all purchases at the chain.

The key to making the Starbucks Card happen was shifting it from a visionary idea to a very practical, grounded project. When he described the vision, "eyes would glaze over." Coworkers literally said things like, "That's never going to work." So to make the idea more palatable, he "sold what was easy to sell—the first version of the project."

The status quo thinking then works in your favor. Once the card is in place, it's a thousand times easier to add a business-to-business program (offering it to companies as an employee benefit) or adding auto-replenishment from a charge card.

To make sure that approvals were a one-way street (no backtracking) Bill actually got signatures of people committing to the project. That was his goal—to get the signature, to make the sale.

Tactic: Hire a Librarian

Moving a soft innovation through an organization involves more than getting buy-in. It also involves a lot of paper.

As we become more networked and our organizations become more complex (it's never totally clear who does what) we end up with more forms, more flowcharts and more confusion. Every decision must be distributed to the right people. Complex systems inevitably get more complex, and tracking the flow of information and the support systems that go with it is critical.

Software engineers figured this out a long time ago. Before we had electronic networks, large-scale software-programming efforts always had a human librarian. If you were a programmer working on a specific section of code, you'd go to the librarian, check out that section and work on it. While you were doing your work, no one else could touch your section of code. Then you'd check it back in and the librarian would assemble all the pieces for testing.

So why not do that with your project? Appoint a librarian

and channel all the information, decisions, agendas and meetings through him. By tracking who knows what and who owes what and who decides what, you'll go faster and won't get sidetracked.

Tactic: Paint a Portrait of the Future

Denigrating the status quo makes a lot of people uncomfortable. It feels disloyal. It's negative.

The flip side of this is a lot more exciting. You get to paint a portrait of the future.

Sometimes the portrait is a story. "Imagine what happens when everyone in America has Internet access—and they all start their day in the same place." "Imagine what happens when the classified ads are replaced by a nationwide electronic auction system." These scenarios allow you to build successes upon successes. You can draw a road map, making it clear how your organization wins when the innovations you're describing actually occur.

It gets better when you make the portrait more vivid. Segway and Apple both used a video to show what the world would be like if their innovations caught on. It doesn't matter that both videos were used for years without alteration. It doesn't matter that the future portrayed in the videos hasn't happened. What's important is that it gave the group a shared vision. It gave people permission to get excited. It allowed others to contribute their riffs (the positive ones) on how to make the vision even more likely to occur.

This is what spreadsheets are for. Not because they're an accurate rendering of your profits in three years. Because they concretize the future.

When Vince Barabba at General Motors was trying to sell the organization on OnStar, he was lucky enough to find an engineer who was able to make the goal vivid. "Let me see if I get this. You're building a cash register into the car and every time somebody uses it, the cash register rings for GM?" Suddenly, it got a lot easier to overcome hurdles.

Special Bonus Tactic: Avoid Really Bad PowerPoint

It doesn't matter whether you're trying to champion an idea at a church or a school or a Fortune 100 company, you're probably going to use PowerPoint.

PowerPoint was developed by engineers as a tool to help them communicate with the marketing department—and vice versa. It's a remarkable tool because it allows for very dense verbal communication. Yes, you could send a memo, but no one reads anymore. As our companies are getting faster and faster, we need a way to quickly communicate ideas from one group to another. Enter PowerPoint.

PowerPoint could be the most powerful tool on your computer. But it's not. Countless soft innovations fail because their champions use PowerPoint the way Microsoft wants them to, instead of the right way.

> Communication is the transfer of emotion.

Communication is about getting others to adopt your point of view, to help them understand why you're excited (or sad, or optimistic or whatever else you are). If all you want to do is create a file of facts and figures, then cancel the meeting and send in a report.

Our brains have two sides. The right side is emotional and musical. The left side is focused on dexterity and hard data. When you show up to give a presentation, people use both parts of their brains. They use the right side to judge the way you talk, the way you dress and your body language. Often, people come to a conclusion about your presentation by the time you're on the second slide. After that, it's often too late for your bullet points to do you much good.

You can wreck the communication process with lousy logic or unsupported facts, but logic is not enough. You can't complete it without emotion.

> Champions must sell—both to internal audiences and to the outside world.

If everyone in the room agreed with you, you wouldn't need to do a presentation, would you? You could save a lot of time by printing out a one-page project report and delivering it to each person. No, the reason we do presentations is to make a point, to sell one or more ideas.

If you believe in your idea, sell it. Make your point as hard as you can and get what you came for. Your audience will thank you for it, because deep down, *we all want to be sold.*

Four Components to a Great Presentation

First, make yourself cue cards. Don't put them on the screen. Put them in your hand. Now, you can use the cue cards you made to make sure you're saying what you came to say.

Second, make slides that reinforce your words, not repeat them. Create slides that demonstrate, with emotional proof, that what you're saying is true, not just accurate.

Talking about pollution in Houston? Instead of giving me four bullet points of EPA data, why not show me a photo of a bunch of dead birds, some smog and even a diseased lung? This is cheating! It's unfair! It works.

Third, create a written document. A leave behind. Put in as many footnotes or details as you like. Then when you start your presentation, tell the audience that you're going to give them all the details of your presentation after it's over, so they don't have to write down everything you say. Remember, the presentation is to make an emotional sale. The document is the proof that helps the intellectuals in your audience accept the idea that you've sold them emotionally.

Important: Don't hand out the written stuff at the beginning! If you do, people will read the memo while you're talking and ignore you. Instead, your goal is to get them to sit back, trust you and take in the emotional and intellectual points of your presentation.

Fourth, create a feedback cycle. If your presentation is for a project approval, hand people a project approval form and get them to fill it out, so there's no ambiguity at all about what they've agreed to.

The reason you give a presentation is to make a sale, so make it. Don't leave without a yes, or at the very least, a commitment to a date or to future deliverables.

Bullets Are for the NRA

Here are the five rules you need to remember to create amazing PowerPoint presentations:

1. No more than six words on a slide. *Ever.* There is no presentation so complex that this rule needs to be broken.

2. No cheesy images. Use professional stock photo images.

3. No dissolves, spins or other transitions.

4. Sound effects can be used a few times per presentation, but never use the sound effects that are built into the program. Instead, rip sounds and music from CDs and leverage the Proustian effect this can have. If people start bouncing up and down to the Grateful Dead, you've kept them from falling asleep, and you've reminded them that this isn't a typical meeting you're running.

5. Don't hand out printouts of your slides. They don't work without you there.

The home run is easy to describe: You put up a slide. It triggers an emotional reaction in the audience. They sit up and want to know what you're going to say that fits in with that image. Then, if you do it right, every time they think of what you said, they'll see the image (and vice versa).

Sure, this is different from the way everyone else does it. But everyone else is busy defending the status quo (which is easy) and you're busy championing brave new innovations, which is difficult.

The Three Biggest PowerPoint Mistakes

PowerPoint has one function: to communicate with your audience. Unfortunately, rather than communicating, PowerPoint is used to accomplish three things, none of which leads to a good presentation.

Most people use PowerPoint as a TelePrompTer. Think of all the presentations you've been to where the presenter actually reads from the slides. Did your audience really have to come all this way to a meeting to listen to you read the slides? Why not just send them over by fax?

The second misuse is to provide a written, cover-your-ass record of what was presented. By handing out the slides after the meeting (or worse, before), the presenter is avoiding the job of writing a formal report and is making sure that she can point to the implicit approval she earned by having the meeting.

The third misguided use is to focus on ensuring that your audience remembers everything you said. Sort of like reading your slides, but better. After all, if you read your slides, and then give the audience a verbatim transcript of what you read, what could be wrong with that? A memo, though, is faster, easier and more direct.

Tactic: Take Responsibility

Of course, you don't always have to take responsibility. Some-times, people *give* it to you!

When you're a champion, you have a powerful tool available to you. You can lower your voice, pause, look everyone right in the eye and say, "I take responsibility for making this happen."

When you do that, people will be stunned. It's so unusual to hear that said in most organizations. If you've worked the ful-crum properly (and people already believe you can handle the project) then it's more than likely to lead people into trusting you enough to give you a shot. When Rich Gioscia was director of design at Sony, he created a new kind of remote control, one that would be easier to find if you dropped it behind the couch. People were skeptical. But then he and his team stood up and said, "We're the design team—we're going to put our reputation on the line with this." It moved the project one step further down the pike.

But isn't this a risky tactic?

Nope. Because if you don't say that, and the project fails, the skeptics are going to be coming after you anyway. If you don't take responsibility, they're going to be working hard to give it to you (a nice way of saying they'll try to blame you).

On the other hand, if you take responsibility from the very beginning, people are going to root for you and are far more likely to forgive you if everything blows up. The one thing most

CEOs have in common is *not* that they never failed. It's that they failed often, but took responsibility for it when they did.

Tactic: Use the Tricks of Hollywood

Who's good at persuading people by using emotion? Actors. As a champion, you're an actor. Your goal is to paint an emotional portrait of two futures—one with your free prize, and one without.

So why not use the tricks that directors use to make their actors more persuasive? Setting the stage, for starters. Don't slump into your boss's office to present your great idea midway between two tightly scheduled meetings.

Presuming you've followed the process—laid the groundwork, received buy-in from critical constituencies, built a prototype and created an emotional PowerPoint presentation—now's the time to do the big presentation. Do it right.

Do it in the boardroom. Rearrange the reception area. Rent a small room at a local restaurant. Do it after work and project your slides on the outside wall of the building. Serve great snacks. Arrange the room so that you're in the right spot, not jammed against the wall.

If your innovation is going to transform your company for years to come, it's worth a few hours of effort to make the presentation count. You never get a second chance on that first impression.

Tactic: Understand the Power of the Schedule

Most of us spend our working lives on projects, but very few people have any clue at all about how to manage them. Specifically, we're horrible at managing time.

If you had unlimited time, it would be easy. But you don't. You never do. You never have enough. And time is money. Positive thinking doesn't create more time. Good intentions don't create more time. Champions understand that being hardheaded about time is the single best way to make the innovation happen.

Steve McConnell wrote a book called *Software Project Survival Guide*, which has nothing to do with software and everything to do with projects. The entire book can be summed up in two charts:

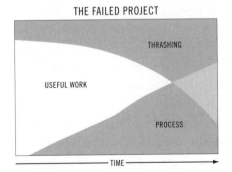

THE FAILED PROJECT

THRASHING

USEFUL WORK

PROCESS

TIME

THE SUCCESSFUL PROJECT

As a project proceeds, decisions are made, parts are bought, relationships are forged. At every step along the way, making a change gets more expensive. As deadlines approach and more and more people are involved, it gets *exponentially* more expensive to do anything new.

In the failed project, you can see that the developers were greedy. They skimped on process early on, so they could get to the useful work. Alas, that decision comes back to haunt them. As the project gets more mired in thrashing (changes, arguments, midcourse corrections and lost information) they try to add more process back in, but soon the combination of overhead, bureaucracy and frustration leads the project to its doom.

The most obvious symptom of a failed project is that management tries to add a lot of people and money at the end (now that it is important and failure is expensive). This never works, because more people (who create more thrashing) actually slow a project down rather than fix it.

The successful project, on the other hand, feels like one of Aesop's fables. The developers invest in process from the start, and allocate themselves plenty of time to thrash—at the beginning! Then the process takes over, the thrashing subsides and the amount of useful work is quite large, plenty big enough to get to the end of the project.

Do all your invention at the beginning. Get all your approvals early on. Lock the thing, throw away the key and spend the last third of the project doing nothing but building it and testing it.

SMART PROJECT

In fact, groups almost always do precisely the opposite. We postpone the difficult decisions, the difficult meetings and the difficult approvals to the end. We wait until the deadline to do what we should have done at the very beginning.

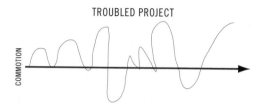

Architects even have a name for this. They call it a *charrette*. It's the last-minute hoo-ha that occurs right before a presentation is due—where all the great juices flow and the good decisions are made. Except, of course, they're not always good decisions.

This is why everything costs more than it should. This is why every champion should read Steve's book and follow his advice. Have your *charrette* at the beginning, not at the end. Discipline is difficult, but it's free and it's worth it.

Bringing It Together: Working the System at FedEx

If you've walked through a big U.S. city, one thing you've probably noticed is how many FedEx trucks there are. If you've walked through a big city with a FedEx envelope in your hand looking for a FedEx office, you've probably wondered why you can't give it to the FedEx guy driving the truck.

Joe Perrone, retail sales manager for the Eastern region had the same thought. But he did something about it. It occurred to

Joe that he could turn every one of those trucks into a rolling office by cutting a slot in the side of the truck. That way, if you saw a truck (preferably one that was stopped at a light or parked), you could slide your envelope into the slot and go on your way.

Of course, in addition to being convenient, the slot is a rolling advertisement for how easy it is to ship by FedEx.

FedEx thrives by delivering things on time, not by creating fashionable innovations. It's unlikely that management would have been happy if Joe had taken a Skilsaw and started cutting holes in trucks. So he chose to champion the soft innovation through the system.

Joe first approached the corporate identity group. He asked if his slot would affect the FedEx brand (by obscuring the logo, when the slot was cut into trucks). Notice that he *didn't* ask for permission. He didn't say, "I've got this great idea. Do you guys want to do it?" Instead, he asked if they were willing to hear more (if someone else did the work). They agreed.

Next, he asked legal/security for their opinions on the idea; FedEx had to deal with legal issues such as how to handle the unchecked packages once they had custodial care of them. Finally, he cajoled engineering to deal with some logistical questions, such as how to prevent bombs and rain from getting in the slot. They created a slot that was weatherproof and would not allow people to reach inside to grab something.

Joe focused on internal coordination. "If we can solve that

problem," he'd ask, "are you willing to try this?" As each department bought in, he made sure the other departments knew about his progress. Every department had concerns, but none was big enough to make them refuse the project.

Yes, he was helped by the fact that senior management was in favor of the idea, but he knew that he couldn't *force* anyone to say yes. The key was that he championed it, step by step, until there was no one left to object. Along the way, he kept painting the portrait of the future (increased convenience, free marketing) and emphasizing the lack of cost to give it a try.

Were senior FedEx people dying to come to his meetings? Not at all. So he pushed ahead on his own, getting a prototype built as fast as possible, making it easier for everyone to visualize it, and even more important, establishing that this thing was going to happen—so people ought to get in now, before it was too late to give their input.

My favorite part of this story is how prosaic it is. Nothing revolutionary, nothing flashy. Just a step-by-step championing process that got the job done.

Bringing It Together: Voting for Stamps

Start with a simple soft innovation: Let U.S. consumers celebrate the end of the millennium by voting for which events will be commemorated with a stamp.

Azeez Jaffer came up with the idea while on a business trip, then became a champion for making it happen.

He realized that having a deadline would make it possible to push it through the many layers of approval at the Postal Service. At every step, he used the urgency of the upcoming millennium to make it happen.

Jaffer started with his creative "tiger team," a group of 3 or 4 senior people with whom he discussed the concept. They used "March to the Millennium" as the working project title—giving something a name makes it more real. After they had ironed out some of the initial details, they went into seclusion for a few days with their cross-functional team; there, they decided how to market their project (create voting ballots for mail, e-mail, schools) and develop it. For example, the group decided that the committee should dictate the choices for the first few decades, since most people wouldn't know what to choose as significant from 1920 or 1930.

Notice that Jaffer worked out a framework early, and made sure to involve people from across the organization. The next step was more difficult. Jaffer had to work with the Citizens' Stamp Advisory Committee, a group that normally takes 5–7 *years* to go from idea to stamp. Without a deadline, he wouldn't have had a chance. "This idea was completely counterculture," he said. "I was thrown out of the room," he joked. The committee and people were used to working through a process of years, not three to five months.

Once this hurdle was addressed, Jaffer beefed up his vision of the future. Specifically, he knew that management was very focused on the bottom line. "We ran the numbers, and it was clear this would add fifty million dollars to the bottom line," he explained.

The next level of the organization cared much more about how it looked to the outside world. So he sold them on the role of the project in history, and showed them that this was a program that would show the world the USPS was being progressive even if it failed. (He convinced the transportation head in the same way: "This is what it's all about. Your kids and grandkids will read about this.")

Jaffer didn't have to convince everyone. In fact, he walked away from some people when they showed the first signs of resistance. How'd he know which people he could walk away from? "Because I knew which would make or break me." As the project gained steam, the fact that he was willing to leave people out actually gave him more power, not less.

Result? He made his numbers (it was the most successful rollout in USPS history). He got promoted. And he was the Man of the Year for the American Stamp Dealers Association and was on the cover of *Promo* magazine.

If the USPS can move that quickly, so can you.

Bringing It Together:
Saving Lives, Saving Money

Dr. Peter Pronovost came up with a simple soft innovation that is revolutionizing the intensive care ward. But it wouldn't have happened if he wasn't also a champion.

In July 2001, he designed a safety program that could be rolled out to different hospitals. Communication, it turns out, was the fundamental challenge to improving care—not machines, not education, not access to medicine. For example, even immediately after rounds, only 10 percent of doctors said they understood what they would need to do to treat a particular patient.

Dr. Pronovost's insight: He developed a checklist of goals and treatments that has cut the average length of stay in the ICU in half. Predictably, there was resistance from the doctors and nurses. Doctors didn't want their autonomy threatened by a checklist. Nurses didn't want to have to overrule doctors and get in trouble.

Pronovost realized that he had to sell a solution—that inventing one wasn't enough. He sat down with groups of doctors. He asked them if it was acceptable to harm patients. By painting a portrait of a better future (one without harm to patients) he made it easier for them to swallow the new tactics.

Then he took responsibility. He told the nurses that they

could page him if there was ever a doctor who wasn't support-ing the checklist. To date, he has never been paged. Merely an-nouncing his responsibility was sufficient.

Measuring the results finalized his argument. By showing its impact, he made his innovation into a permanent policy, and it's spreading to other hospitals. And Dr. Pronovost has been promoted to head a new innovation center at Johns Hopkins.

What's in It for You?

In the old days, a journeyman was a skilled craftsman who didn't depend on guild protection to get work. He journeyed from job to job, carrying his tools and doing great work on his own. If you learn how to champion projects, you become a journeyman, a self-contained secret weapon.

Once you become a champion, you're guaranteed success. Yes, it's true, your company won't need you forever. Companies grow and evolve and most of them get to the point where they're too stuck to want to do much that is new. But every day, thousands of companies go looking for a champion, someone who has the skills and confidence to make something happen. Once you know how to champion a project, you're set for life, regardless of where you happen to be working.

Why You Should Build Cheap Stuff

After three years, women's professional soccer has folded. It cost $100 million to discover that high-profile women's soccer wasn't going to make a profit (not right now, not right here). Does that mean that soccer can't work for women? Of course not. But it didn't take three or four years to launch major league baseball—it took decades. If they had spent only $10 million, they'd still be around today, with enough money in the bank to last another twenty years. If you've got a great product, realize that nearly all the free prizes start out cheap and small.

Of course, if hype is what you need to beat the word of mouth (and you can afford it) it's not a bad idea. Madonna's new kids' book launched in more than fifty countries simultaneously—to horrible reviews. There's no way she would have made the best-seller lists using an ideavirus—an idea that spreads exponentially—because her book won't become a classic. On the other hand, most true successes seem to come out of nowhere, not from the red-hot center of hype.

It's tempting to try to short-circuit the system, to front-load your project with plenty of cash and plenty of staff. It works for Madonna. But nine times out of ten, it's the underfunded but truly wonderful free prize that breaks through. No one expected Alice Sebold's debut novel to become a massive best seller. It wasn't hype that did it. Instead, it was the person-to-person ideavirus that spread the word and sold the book.

The Segway Paradox

The message of this chapter should have been clear: Projects don't happen without champions and you can become a champion if you pick a project of the right size.

Often, though, the innovations that seem worth doing are the ones we are unable to do. They are beyond our reach, too big for us to handle. That doesn't mean you should give up, nor does it mean you have no choice but to aim for the impossible ones.

Instead, you must focus on the high-leverage projects you do have the power to champion. It doesn't have to be a brand makeover, a technology revolution or a major pricing overhaul. It can be a simple change to the way your people answer the phone, or a different way of talking about the benefits of your product.

The point is *not* to be perfect, or brilliant or awe inspiring. The goal is to start down the path of searching for the free prize, and build a reputation as someone who can work all three points of the fulcrum. As you gain experience and skill in being a champion, the magnitude of the projects will naturally increase. Dean Kamen didn't start with the Segway. Neither will you.

FIVE QUESTIONS

1. Is this project worth doing?

2. When I ask for help with the project I want to do, will people say, "she's the one to champion this"?

3. Are we disciplined enough to do all our thrashing at the beginning of a project?

4. If we had unlimited time, would this be easy? If so, how do we manage the time we do have?

5. Could it be done cheaper and quicker?

Going to the Edges—Finding the Innovation

Okay, let's say you're sold on what you've read so far. You realize that a free prize really is free, it's essential and it won't happen unless you champion it. Your next question is the one you've been asking all along: "Where do I find one?"

One of the great myths is that great ideas are worth a lot. In a world filled with nondisclosure agreements, secret meetings and jealous inventors, it's easy to believe that you need to spend a really long time searching before you find an idea worth building.

David Owen proved this wrong once and for all. He runs a Web site called idea-a-day.com. Not surprisingly, they publish (by e-mail) a new idea every day. For free. Not all the ideas are perfect. Some of the ideas are great, naturally, while others are pretty dodgy.

What I love is how many ideas there are. What I love is the fact that every single day for more than one thousand days, a new idea has shown up in my e-mail box, free of charge. This is proof positive that we've got more ideas than we know what to do with. Proof that *your* idea, no matter how great it is, can't possibly be much better than all of the ideas that have been distributed by idea-a-day.com.

The lessons of idea-a-day.com are simple. First, stop keeping your idea a secret. Ideas in secret die. They need light and air or they starve to death. The more people you share your idea with, the more likely it is to become real.

The second lesson is even more important—it's not the idea that matters, it's what you do with it. The real challenge (and the real skill) comes from championing your idea, shepherding it through the system and turning it into a reality.

Of course, you still need an idea to start with. And that's what this section of the book is about.

Brainstorming Is Fine, but It's Not What You Need

Brainstorming is a mystical, magical event. It's designed to quiet the mind and allow your innately great ideas to surface. By challenging those around you to remain positive, and by creating an environment of enormous productive energy, it allows you to reach your full potential.

Brainstorming is about nonlateral thinking. About finding

the odd connections that help you jump from one reality to another.

You've tried it, I'm sure. It doesn't work (at least not at your company).

It doesn't work because people can't keep their mouths shut. When an idea gets too close to sounding real, your colleagues are overcome with the urge to pick at it, because they believe that if they don't, they'll be on the hook to implement it later. People hold back during brainstorming sessions because they understand that if they say something now, they might have to do it later.

It doesn't work because your company doesn't need to be nonlateral. You don't need to have ideas that are startling in their originality (I'm sure you've already got those). What you need is the guts to do the things you need to do.

Would you want emergency medical care or even architectural services from someone who relied on techniques that are as intermittent (okay, flaky) as brainstorming can be? Not me. It's too unreliable, it's performed by people who haven't trained at it and aren't very good, and it's far too easy to sabotage.

I want to be really clear—the truly great, off-the-edge sorts of ideas come from people who have trained their creative edge, who are artists in the art of creativity. I wouldn't trade this gift (talent?) for anything, and I'm not diminishing it. I am, however, tired of hearing people say that they're not able to come up with good ideas, that they're stuck, that they don't have a gift so they have no choice but to stick with what they've got. That's nonsense.

Here's the proof you need to believe what I'm saying: Psychologist Paul Paulus has studied brainstorming for fourteen years at the University of Texas. He's discovered that four individuals working on their own come up with about twice as much output as the same four people brainstorming together.

We need an alternative to brainstorming. Something that everyone responsible for creating a free prize can use (that's all of us). Something that always works, that generates ideas that can be improved upon and that is transparent, not magical.

Introducing Edgecraft

Edgecraft is a methodical, measurable process that allows individuals and teams to inexorably identify the soft innovations that live on the edges of what already exists. Because the process of edgecraft is similar to many of the skills we're already good at, your organization is much more likely to embrace it. Because it allows us to gradually move to a best available answer, it's more robust as well.

Once you start down the path to a solution using edgecraft, your peers can help you move ever closer to the edge. The goals of the process are obvious and there's no magic involved.

Edgecraft is easy to learn and can work in any domain, commercial or social. It can be done quickly or over long periods of time. And you can even do it by yourself. In fact, people who brainstorm in the shower are often doing edgecraft without realizing it.

> Edgecraft isn't hard, but some people find it difficult. To succeed, you have to have the guts to go all the way to the edges.

Edgecraft Is a Straightforward Process

1. Find an edge—a free prize that has been shown to make a product or service remarkable.

2. Go all the way to that edge—as far from the center as the consumers you are trying to reach dare you to go.

You must go all the way to the edge. Accepting second best doesn't make sense. Running a restaurant where the free prize is your slightly attractive waitstaff won't work—they've got to be supermodels or weight lifters or identical twins. You only create a free prize when you go all the way to the edge and create something remarkable.

Before you learn how to do edgecraft, you must accept the fact that the edges of a problem aren't always obvious. Because the edge you're seeking is not the primary reason for being, you've got to see it out of the corner of your eye. It's not always clear exactly what would make your product or service significantly more remarkable, until you embrace the fact that the problem you're trying to solve isn't the problem you think you have!

Sometimes you don't discover the problem you're solving until after you've solved it—it's not always a top-down process. Someone creates something weird or neat or quirky or fun and the marketplace embraces it. You don't create a better restaurant by serving better food. You can do it by serving remarkable food, or having a remarkable location or a remarkably famous chef. You don't build a better car by building a faster car. You do it by building the fastest car, or the least polluting car, or the biggest car.

People Don't Buy a Watch (Just) to Tell the Time

If you spent more than $10 on a watch, you're not only buying the time. You can "buy the time" with a more accurate device than anything mankind could have conceived (until a couple of decades ago) for a few dollars at the drugstore. Making an accurate watch isn't hard at all.

Which means that a *better* watch is not a more accurate watch. Spending $100 or $1,000 for a watch that's more accurate or more durable is stupid. So, assuming that most people with expensive watches aren't stupid, what's going on?

Turns out that you also want a watch that's beautiful, slim, lightweight, handsome, Russian, Swiss, retro, clunky, prestigious, expensive, glamorous, almost invisible, without computerized parts, with a second hand, with a pedigree and with a sense of humor. It turns out that a Franck Muller watch (for example, the Perpetual Calendar with Retrograde Monthly Equation, Tourbillon and Split-Sec Chronometer) could easily cost more than $10,000, without fancy jewelry. Muller figured out what his customers want. He doesn't sell watches. He sells Tourbillons with Complications.

So, if you're committed to selling just the time (whatever "time" means for your product or service), then this book won't do you much good and you're doomed to slow growth and commodity pricing. If, however, you embrace the fact that people rarely buy what they *say* they're buying, you have a chance to create a free prize. *The free prize is the element that transcends the utility of the original idea and adds a special, unique element worth paying extra for, worth commenting on.*

After buying a Muller complication, what are the chances you'll say to a friend, "Wanna see my watch?" The product *is* the marketing.

> The goal of edgecraft is to find the free prize worth paying for.

Is It the Cookie or the Fortune?

The rest of this chapter is dedicated to helping you figure out your prize. It's not a complete list of tactics and possibilities, but it's a starting point.

By now, your product is right near the center, far from the edges. Over time, your management, your retailers, your customers, have all conspired to smooth things out and push you to the middle. Most companies focus on creating average products for average people. The goal in edgecraft is figuring out what some people *really* want to buy, what they want to talk about, and then giving it to them.

So, what you need to do is add a second benefit, a new edge, something your product or service does that is truly remarkable. You can only do that by going to the edges.

The Edges

The rest of this chapter can't help but be sort of random. There's no way I can describe each and every edge. Instead, I'm going to start by listing a few dozen edges, hoping that this will give you a head start. The categories I've invented are by no means mutually exclusive. Later, I'll describe some of the edges in detail (with examples) so you can get a feel for how each edge works in practice.

Here's an abridged list of edges*:

Edges That Create Conversations

USE A NETWORK TO CONNECT ONE USER
OF YOUR PRODUCT OR SERVICE WITH OTHERS
  instant messaging
  meetup.com, user groups
  Federal Express

CREATE EVENTS THAT BRING IN NEW USERS AND CONNECT OLD ONES
  school night at the Apple store

MAKE AN INVISIBLE SERVICE VISIBLE
  labeling food organic
  putting yellow ribbons on trees

CREATE A SENSATION
  Deloitte & Touche's Bullfighter software

Edges That Confound Expectations

MAKE A VISIBLE PRODUCT INVISIBLE
  braces on teeth

*Bonus: An annotated, revised version of the following is found in the latest version of the endnotes, available for free at www.freeprizeinside.com.

USE A LOT OF THE USER'S TIME
three-hour tasting menu

Edges That Satisfy Real Needs *and* Wants

SAVE THE USER AN ENORMOUS AMOUNT OF TIME
Federal Express
instant lube jobs

FORTIFY AN UNEXPLORED AREA
Vitamin Water
Gore-Tex
aromatherapy skin lotion

Edges That Address Overlooked Senses

MAKE A PRODUCT SENSUAL OR ASCETIC
Krispy Kreme
Ultralight camping equipment

GREAT DESIGN/CHEESY DESIGN
Schrager Hotels
Jack in the Box

INTERACTIVE/STATIC
Hypermarkets
point-and-shoot disposable cameras

Edges That Address Overlooked Markets

TARGET GEEKS OR LAGGARDS
TiVo
WebTV
www.dynamism.com

CREATE A NEW FORMAT OR RESCUE AN OLD ONE
LP (vinyl) sales increased last year
CDs fell while downloads increased

Edges That Highlight the Free Prize

MAKE A PRODUCT THAT IS VERY SAFE OR VERY DANGEROUS
antibacterial wipes for kids
helicopter skiing

LEAVE SOMETHING OUT
MTV's Unplugged
freon-free air conditioners
VO-free paint

OVERBUILD FOR THE USER'S NEEDS
Patagonia
Buzz Rickson nylon jackets

MAXIMIZE OR MINIMIZE EXTERNALITIES
>   Car stereos that can be heard down the block
>   hypoallergenic cosmetics

HELP A CONTROVERSIAL CAUSE OR HURT ONE
>   Donald Wildmon's campaign to ban profanity from radio
>   bars that refuse to ban smoking

MAKE THE INVISIBLE PRODUCT VISIBLE
>   white headphones on the iPod

Edges That Change the Structure of the Market

TREAT DIFFERENT CUSTOMERS DIFFERENTLY
>   American Express's Centurion Card
>   Rao's Restaurant

TREAT DIFFERENT CUSTOMERS THE SAME
>   no reservations at Johnny's

DISRUPT OR EMBRACE INDUSTRY STANDARDS
>   school vouchers
>   MySQL

LEVERAGE AN OLD SALES FORCE OR BUILD A NEW SALES FORCE
>   selling new products at Avon
>   Travelocity.com

SELL TO A NEW MARKET/SELL A NEW PRODUCT TO YOUR MARKET
  McKinsey targeting nonprofits
  Amazon selling food and sporting goods

FIND AN ALTERNATIVE RETAIL CHANNEL
  Cranium board game at Starbucks

MAKE A PRODUCT MORE CONVENIENT OR LESS CONVENIENT
  Parmalat shelf-stable milk in a box
  fresh rice noodles

MINIMIZE OR MAXIMIZE THE PACKAGING
  generic cereal in a bag
  premium prewashed salad in a bag
  the first printing of this book

SELL BY SUBSCRIPTION
  Revival energy bars and shakes

MOVE RETAIL OUTLETS TO NONRETAIL LOCATIONS/
PUT YOUR NONRETAIL OUTLET IN A MALL
  McDonald's in jail
  H&R Block

TAKE ADVANTAGE OF UNUSUAL TIMING
Launch rivalry merchandise hours after a football game (like T-shirts with "Auburn's tiger mascot strangling the Alabama elephant," as *The Wall Street Journal* wrote)

UNBUNDLE IT
CFO-for-hire services

OPEN ALL THE TIME/RARELY OPEN
Kang Suh twenty-four-hour Korean restaurant
Halloween superstores

BECOME UBIQUITOUS (OR RARE)
Dasani water
Yoo-hoo

Edges Worth Noticing

MAKE BORING THINGS SEEM UNBORING
Red Bull

MAKE IT SMELL
Montana Mills bread

OBSESS WITH CLEANLINESS
JetBlue

ADD SOME GRITTINESS
>   Buca di Beppo

FAKE SOME SURLINESS
>   Carnegie Deli

ADD SOME UNEXPECTED FRIENDLINESS
>   receptionist at Kodak

SUPERSIZE OR MICROSIZE IT
>   Costco
>   tiny video cameras

PUT THINGS TOGETHER/TAKE THINGS APART
>   peanut butter and jelly
>   CD players and processors

Obsess on One Element

ADD MORE POWER, OR REMOVE WEIGHT
SO YOU DON'T NEED EXTRA POWER
>   Chevy SSR truck with a three hundred-horse power
>   engine
>   Lotus Elise

LEAVE INGREDIENTS OUT/PUT INGREDIENTS IN
> Betty Crocker cakes
> waterproof laptops

MAKE IT MUCH BIGGER OR MUCH SMALLER
> WPP ad-agency network
> one-person ad agency

MAKE THE PERMANENT DISPOSABLE
OR MAKE THE DISPOSABLE REUSABLE
> Disposable digital cameras
> $2000 fancy pens

ADD COLOR, LOSE COLOR
> Keds
> Giorgio Armani

TALK IN A DIFFERENT TONE OF VOICE

MAKE IT A PARODY
> Silk soy milk box

MAKE A SILLY THING SERIOUS
> Kubrick collectible Lego

BECOME THE EXPERT IN A NEW FIELD
> Jakob Nielsen

MAKE FORMAL UNIFORMS CASUAL/MAKE INFORMAL DRESS FORMAL
    waiters at Spago
    airport guards in Italy

LIVE YOUR LIFE IN PUBLIC/REFUSE TO TALK TO THE MEDIA
    Joi Ito
    Thomas Pynchon

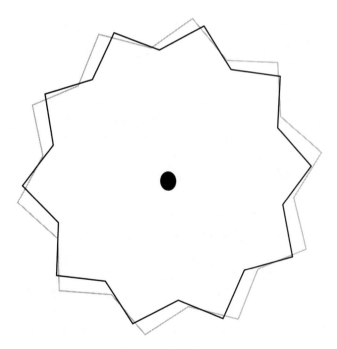

You're the circle, caught in the center of a web of boring. The goal of edgecraft is to pick an edge (there are hundreds to choose from) and go all the way with it—even a little further than that if you can. Moving a little is expensive and useless. Moving a lot is actually cheaper in the long run and loaded with wonderful possibilities. It's easy (but pointless) to keep your store open another thirty minutes a day. It's more difficult (but possibly a fantastic strategy) to keep your store open twenty-four hours a day. Little changes *cost* you. Big changes *benefit* you by changing the game.

When a version of your product moves from its boring position in the center to the more interesting world at (not near, but *at*) the edge, you will discover new customers—and they'll discover you. This isn't about inventing entire new markets through original invention. Instead, it's about adding a new dimension to the solution you've already created—making it far more appealing to a much bigger market.

When Avon turned the breast cancer walkathon into a movement, something that transcended both gender and health, they ended up raising millions of dollars more for research. Not by changing the research, but by going to the edge and having their appeal reach far more people.

I can't help you find the perfect idea. The good news is that you're already capable of finding a great idea. Not by using a random brainstorming process, but by iterating through the edges until you find one that will work for you.

Brainstorming might create the occasional breakthrough, but edgecraft can build a process that inexpensively and quickly churns out lots of ideas—good, and sometimes great, ideas—that you can rapidly implement to make something happen.

Successful edgecraft comes down to two things: Pick an edge that matters to your consumer and figure out how to get right to it.

Use Edgecraft to Find a Free Prize, Not to Create Differentiation

Differentiation is the act of making your products different from the competition (and each other) so that people pick you. But differentiation is selfish. It assumes that people are interested enough in your field to seek you out, to compare the options and to make a smart choice. When Apple introduced a third video-editing program (priced between their expensive model and their free one) they were being introspective, not providing a new free prize.

Differentiation is a zero-sum, advertising-based game. In fact, the only thing that leads to real growth is person-to-person conversation, word of mouth. Or better, an ideavirus. And these only come about when you do something truly remarkable. Differentiation is not, by itself, remarkable. To be Purple, you have to be more than different. You must be extreme. You must live on the edge.

Case Study: Windham Ski Area

Windham is located near the more famous Hunter Mountain, a few hours from Manhattan. It's a nice little ski area that would like to do better. Until recently, Windham's focus was on how to make it a better ski area for *most* people. Better lifts, better snow, better equipment. Of course, this is a losing battle, because if I want great skiing I can go to Vermont or even Utah for just a little more money (though it takes more time). Windham will never be the best, most remarkable ski area for people who care about skiing.

But, of course, we pick ski areas for lots of reasons that have nothing to do with skiing. And we certainly don't *talk* about ski areas just because of the skiing. So now, Windham is busy figuring out how to go to the edges. They're exploring the idea of building the best beginner's ski school in the world (why not do it indoors, with a treadmill-type device?), the best chili and Mexican restaurant at any ski area on the East Coast, the most convenient valet service ever ("Hey Bob, I went to Windham and they took the skis from my car and carried them all the way to the bottom of the lift—for free!") and a hundred other concepts. They can't do them all, but by exploring them one by one, they can isolate the things they have a shot at reaching the edges on . . . and then own them.

What About Price and Value?

Missing from the list of edges are two of the most obvious ones. Offering an astonishingly low price or delivering a product that's an amazing value.

Price is a red herring. If all you do is lower your prices, you haven't created a free prize. What you've done is lowered your profit margins and invited a price war. Lowering your prices without doing anything else is a game for desperate people lacking in imagination.

This is a very different strategy from creating an engine of high value. The most famous example is Wal-Mart. Wal-Mart didn't settle for announcing an everyday-low-pricing policy. Instead, they built an organization that makes a huge profit at the same time it underprices the competition. In the words of Jeff Bezos (who has built a similar organization), "There are two kinds of companies—those that work to raise prices and those that work to lower them."

Trader Joe's sells more than $2 billion worth of food a year (with sales per square foot that dwarf the competition) by using a similar engine. Since almost everything in the store is sold with a private label, Trader Joe's can commission high-quality goods but sell them for a fraction of what the same items, branded, would cost.

The list of successful high-value marketers is short but lustrous. Companies like Southwest and Dell and Foxtons (in the

United Kingdom) and Naxos have done well for themselves and their customers by selling value, not discounts. This is great work if you can get it, but too often organizations flirt with this but fail by not getting serious. If you can figure out how to build an engine of value, I beg you to take on the challenge. For the rest of us, fortunately, the other edges await. We must go to other (not price-based) edges and discover other benefits.

What About Quality?

Sell a Better Product seems like a fine slogan. Focusing on quality, on giving consumers more of what they expect, certainly seems like the way to sell more ball bearings, brake linings, cars and watches. That's what most businesses do.

Alas, as we've seen so far, that's no way to grow. You can't achieve rapid growth by being just a bit better than the competition. It's not enough to get people to switch. You'll be ignored in favor of the incumbent. At best, you'll grow as fast as the market does, no more.

Quality is fine for market leaders or those with deep pockets and plenty of time. For the rest of us, real growth comes from somewhere else. Of course your product has to be good enough. Of course shoddy work is unacceptable. But being very good is bad. Being very good is invisible.

The Obvious Edges Don't Usually Work

Most of us are trained to try to make things bigger and faster and newer and cleaner. These seem like edges worth striving for. Continental Airlines runs a billboard that says THE YOUNGEST FLEET, touting the fact that they have the newest jets. (I think JetBlue actually does, but who says you can't lie in advertising?) I'm sure some hotshot marketer at the airline has come to believe that this is Continental's point of differentiation, their USP. The problem, of course, is that no one really cares that Continental's planes are a few months younger. No one notices. You don't walk onto a plane and gasp that the upholstery only has six months' worth of stains on it, not two years' worth.

Attributes like biggest, fastest, tallest, cheapest, easiest, toughest, newest, cleanest and the rest only matter *when they matter to the customer*. Even more important, they only matter when you can deliver an overwhelming distinction. Being somewhere near an edge is a very marketer-centric, self-aware thing that marketers do when they think people care enough to really dig deeply. But since they don't, you don't win by going *near* an edge. You win by going all the way to the limit of the edge and overwhelming it.

If people aren't blown away, they won't talk about it. If they don't talk about it, it doesn't spread fast enough to help you grow.

Some of the Edges

Edge: The Network

This is perhaps the most valuable edge available to most products. In a nutshell, the goal is to build the act of communication right into the product.

My friend Sam Attenberg took those instant-photo booths you find at train stations and added a computer to them so that instead of four pictures on a strip, they printed out sixteen little tiny photos on stickers. The end result? A craze among Japanese teenagers that ended up selling hundreds of millions of dollars' worth of photos! The only reason to buy a set was to share them (for example, by sticking the photos into your friends' autograph books), and the more the photos got shared, the more people bought. Imagine millions of teenage Japanese girls, carrying around their little photo books. It's not that Sam thought it would be a nice addition if people shared the stickers—in fact, the sticker booth doesn't make sense *unless* you share the stickers.

Putting a camera in your cell phone gives you one more way to share. Making a car that people want to talk about because it looks cool is another way to share. (Why buy a Scion if you don't want people to notice it?) When I insisted that people buy my last book in twelve-packs (you got twelve books for the price of three) instead of one book at a time, I was making it obvious to my readers that they should share the other eleven copies with their colleagues. Making a product or service or idea that's easy to share makes it more likely that people will share it.

Sharing doesn't only apply to the spread of intellectual property. You can make it easy for people to compete with each other (the Nathan's hot-dog-eating contest, for example) or easy for them to give your product away (Hallmark cards are always given away, right?).

Derek Sivers's fast-growing CD Baby site features more than one thousand artists who are all busy sending their fans to the site to buy their CDs—and while people are there, of course, they discover the other 999 artists. Amazon made it easy for every customer to become a profit-making affiliate, generating commissions for recommending titles to other people. Netflix puts a coupon in every order, a coupon that's worth giving to a friend to encourage them to become a customer.

Why not build a retail store with Web cams, so your friends can watch (and rate) the clothes you try on—from the safety of their own living rooms? . . .

I used to think that only a special class of products and services (things like Hotmail) could be truly viral. Now, I'm not so sure. Brownie Wise at Tupperware realized something that I didn't—if you make it fun and easy (and profitable) to talk about a product, it's likely that people will.

> If you go all the way to the edge and build communi-
> cation into the use of your product, it instantly be-
> comes remarkable!

Edge: Ergonomics

Like Tom Peters, I'm crazy about good design. And ergonomics is a special case of design.

If you can dramatically increase the performance of your product by rearranging the interface, reordering the buttons or reconfiguring the handle, your most frequent users are going to notice. If your product is important to them, they'll end up using it more, and they're likely to tell their friends about it as well.

The original Palm Pilot broke through as a rare technology hardware success because the user interface was so good and so simple. It cost nothing to put the right buttons in the right place, but it paid off with years of rapid growth. Of course, ergonomics also works for toothpaste (as we learned from the fast growth of the pump) and even Frog Design's extraordinary pipette, which saves lives and time every day.

The astonishing thing is that you can also (occasionally) reach the edges with a *bad* user interface. Unless you've been using the Bloomberg terminal for years, you have to laugh at it. Nearly every serious Wall Street analyst and trader has one on his desk, paying $1,000 a month for the privilege. It's got a large, nonstandard keyboard and (until recently) an ugly, low-resolution screen. It's filled with arcane codes and difficult-to-navigate menus.

Yet, when the Internet came along and offered a wide variety of similar data interfaces for less money, no one switched. The reason is that after investing so much time and sweat in the old interface, no one wanted to give it up and learn a new one. Sort of the way we rally around the QWERTY keyboard, even though it gives us carpal tunnel syndrome!

> Ergonomics that are slightly better are useless. Your product only becomes remarkable when you redefine the user's experience.

Edge: Public Usage

This is a variation of tapping into the network. It means making your invisible product visible by making it clear to other people which brand you're using.

This happened with the Cooper Mini and the Beetle and the Ralph Lauren polo shirt. It could happen with your briefcase (if you sold pink ones) or your barbershop (if you created a cool new hairstyle and offered it free to every senior in the high school).

Toyota's new Scion minivan stands out wherever it goes. The proof of the validity of edges is this: There are two Scion models: the superhip xB and the sort of ordinary xA. The xB outsells the xA hatchback almost two to one.

The Franck Muller watch is another great example. It takes the personal, invisible wristwatch and makes it something worth commenting on. And how did Evian bottled water get Americans to give up the tap? It's easy to carry around (it comes in lightweight plastic bottles), and the first people who did were movie stars, supermodels and magazine executives. People noticed the idea getting sneezed and it spread from there.

Why not move your massage salon's chairs outside in the summer? Or post hundreds of testimonials from your past psychotherapy clients (with names and photos) on your Web site? Not many people would want to volunteer, which is exactly why pulling this off would be so remarkable!

I was talking to an entrepreneur who runs a security guard company—he was frustrated by the slow rate at which his business was gaining market share. While there is plenty of demand (alas) for security guards, he couldn't grow faster than the market. That's obvious when you think about it, since his is a commodity market. Purchasers of security guards are usually looking for the cheapest reliable option—they're not going to switch once they have met their minimum requirements.

What he needed to do, I proposed, was to make his invisible service visible, his unfashionable service fashionable. The best place to start, it seems to me, is with uniforms. Offer guards dressed as Beefeaters or Buckingham Palace guards or paramilitary camo-wearing high-security guards. Or why not a division that only has very friendly, very attractive white-collar guards?

Or male models in latex *Matrix*-type outfits? The minute the service gets noticed, people are more willing to talk about it, to seek it out, to ask for his company.

Edge: Variety

You can make a lot of money selling mixed drinks to slightly inebriated bar-goers. The challenge, of course, is getting them to come to *your* bar instead of the one down the street.

Hi Fi, a bar in the East Village of Manhattan, is usually jammed. The reason? Their jukebox has twenty-six thousand songs in it. By ripping his 1,798 CDs into a custom-built jukebox, Mike Stuto created a remarkable innovation. Remarkable enough that people come in just to listen—it can take as long as three hours for your selection to come up in the queue, the jukebox is so busy. And of course, you'll have a drink (or three) while you wait.

The Amoeba music store in LA takes it a lot further. They sell more than three hundred thousand CDs (new, used and rare), all in stock, all under one roof. Why would anyone go to Virgin? Of course, three hundred thousand might be too many for some people. Hear Music (now part of Starbucks) stocks merely a few thousand discs in their store, but each and every one of them is great (and most from folks you never knew about). Hear succeeds because most record store owners don't have the guts to eliminate 75 percent of their stock.

Mike's Famous Harley-Davidson dealership in Delaware

(the number-one motorcycle dealer in the world) got that way by being big. Lots of new bikes. Lots of used bikes.

At the In-N-Out burger chain (which made more money last year than the entire McDonald's Corporation, by the way), there are only seven items on the menu, including the three flavors of milkshakes.

> Ten percent more stock is invisible. When you have triple or ten times the variety of the competition (or 1 percent of their selection), people will notice.

Edge: Time

You can waste people's time and they'll respond to it! It happens all the time at nightclubs and restaurants. It takes twelve months of waiting to get a custom-made motorcycle from Jesse James.

On the other hand, you also win when you unexpectedly save a bunch of time for the always time-pressed consumer. The FastPass at Disney World was an unqualified success, creating more customer satisfaction (at less cost) than any ride or attraction in the history of the park.

QBNet is the fastest-growing barbershop chain in Japan, and probably the world. Before they came along, the average haircut in Japan took about an hour. There were hot towels, shoulder massages and a long wait for a barber. Kuniyoshi Konishi figured that there had to be a faster (and cheaper) way. He decided to go to the edge of speed.

After seven years, his chain now has two hundred outlets, and has cut the time for a haircut down to ten minutes (and the price from $50 to $8). The key was to focus exclusively on time. The chairs have sensors in them so QB can post an easily noticed color-coded sign outside the shop, showing how long the wait is. There's no shampoo, and the barbers use a centralized vacuum to suck the loose hair away. You don't even pay the barber—customers must use an automated token booth (exact change only) to buy a ticket, which they use to pay for the haircut. By being extremists about saving time while delivering a decent haircut, they became remarkable, profitable and fast-growing.

Balthazar, a restaurant in Manhattan, saves time *and* wastes it. They make the hoi polloi wait, but the beautiful people get an unlisted number and save time by going right to the front of the line. Perversely, this satisfies both groups.

Like most free prizes, this is not an area where half measures are rewarded. If you can lop off a huge chunk of time (or get away with adding a very long wait) then you've got a shot at creating a Purple Cow.

Edge: Packaging

Yes, of course, the package is part of the product, and the free prize can very easily be the package itself. If you bought this book in the cereal box (or my last book in the milk carton) you can see how easy and cheap it is to make a real impact.

The good news is that there's a long, long way to go before the edges of packaging get too crowded. Take a look at Stagnito's *Food and Drug Packaging* magazine to see how much innovation is happening in this industry. Packaging is not a gimmick when it works. Juice boxes, for example, would not be worth seeking out if it weren't for the innovative packaging. The package did more than call attention to the product—it changed the product.

You can go over-the-top by doing more packaging (like Rhino Records and their amazing boxed sets) or you can take an industry where the packaging is a hindrance and strip it away. Audible will sell you only the digitized voice for your favorite book on tape, not the cassette or the box—they have *zero* packaging. By removing the packaging completely, Audible makes it possible to load today's *New York Times* into your iPod in time for your morning commute. By making the packaging for the boxed set so irresistible, Rhino makes downloading the MP3s less attractive.

Edge: Sensuality

Sex sells, even if it's in the form of a Krispy Kreme doughnut. Which sense can you overwhelm with delight? There are now more sushi bars in New York than McDonald's. Sensual sights, smells, tactile experiences or ego trips can spread like wildfire.

The other edge of this attribute is unabashed asceticism. Get close enough and that works too—Wasa Crispbread sells and sells, with an ever-increasing growth curve (they offer no guilt!). If your competitors are all about hedonism, perhaps you should offer precisely the opposite. The Atkins diet, of course, is a miraculous combination of both.

Mexico is jammed with all-in-one resort hotels, but only the Freedom Paradise resort caters to fat people. This is not differentiation, folks. This is creating a free prize (the chance to hang out with other people who find you attractive) for a community that talks to itself.

Edge: Interactivity and Change

In order to buy panty hose, women used to need to go to a department store, wait in line, and then talk to a total stranger about their measurements and crotch preferences. Today, they can go to a supermarket and grab a pair, thanks to L'eggs. L'eggs won that first marketing battle because they took an interactive experience and made it totally unidirectional.

On the other hand, the winner of the Minnesota Typeface Competition did precisely the opposite. The organization's Web site even changes its typeface based on the outside temperature and wind conditions. It takes a static idea and makes it variable.

On Amazon's best-seller list, every listing (of the millions of items) changes every hour. Compare this to your local store, which is the same every time you go. What if the cash register showed shoppers the hottest items in the store—for that day? Convenience stores in Japan are regularly reorganized (several times a day) to match the whims of the shopper of that moment.

Customizing things, making them ever changing and inter-active among groups is a step closer to giving people something to talk about.

> None of these edges are permanent! The standard for edginess changes every day.

Edge: Technology

Moore's law says that every eighteen months, the power of the computer chips you can buy for a dollar doubles. This opens two kinds of opportunity. The first is at the cutting edge. The Xbox or the PlayStation pack supercomputer power in a video game machine. If you could add a supercomputer to your product or service, what would it do? Think about this: Within a few years, we'll be able to predict the weather—accurately—two months ahead of time.

It's easy to believe that this couldn't possibly apply to you and your product, but Hard Manufacturing (yes, they really manufacture . . . the union shop takes steel and bends it into shape, the whole nine yards) is having its greatest success with an old-fashioned crib that has a supersensitive digital scale built in. If autoworkers can install supercomputers, so can you.

The second approach is to take advantage of the cheap part

of the curve—yesterday's technology is always much cheaper. The latest innovation: the $11 digital camera. If computer chips were a penny, how could you use them? Gillette installed RFID digital cameras into displays of their razors in the United Kingdom—and took a picture of every customer.

Edge: Design Aesthetic

Not only the user interface, but the entire user experience is now dictated by design, and design is now on everyone's radar. Design is the single highest-leverage investment you can make— a well-designed product is usually cheaper to make and service than what you're doing now, and it sells better. A true free prize.

Don't tell me it's for the rich. Target thrives with great design. In-N-Out Burger does as well. Once you realize that printing cheesy stuff costs precisely as much as great stuff, that an ugly Web site is as cheap as a beautiful one, you'll understand why great design is available to all of us.

Start with a professional. Considering their skill set, professional designers are a huge bargain. But don't give them a blank sheet of paper. Benchmark yourself from another industry. Give them guidance. "We want to be the Prada bag of socks," for example.

My friend Keith Yamashita has a great design checklist. You can find it in the endnotes.

Of all the edges I know of, embracing amazing design is the easiest, the fastest and the one with the most assured return on investment. We've only touched the tip of the iceberg of what great design can do for a product, a service, a form, even an organization. And of course, "great" design is in the eye of the beholder. What matters is that your design is on the edge, love it or hate it.

Virginia Postrel understands this. In *The Substance of Style*, she puts it quite clearly: "Decoration and adornment are neither higher nor lower than 'real' life. They are part of it."

Haeftling, a German clothing line, understands design even more profoundly. They took the output of convict laborers working at a sweatshop in a prison in Germany, added cutting-edge design and created such a demand that they've been completely sold out for months.

Design doesn't only mean ink on paper, or plastic or steel. Consider:

- The design of David Letterman's teeth or Michael Jackson's nose.

- The sound of Howlin' Wolf's voice or the click of the iPod.

- The feel of the Porsche steering wheel or the best Nokia phones.

- The smell of the lodge at the Sagamore Resort in Lake George (yuck) or the bakery at Balthazar in Manhattan.

- The taste of the watercress salad at Sripraphai or a Chupa Chups lollipop.

Edge: Safety

Baby boomers want to live forever. Safety matters. Or does it? Kiteboarding is one of the fastest-growing sports in the country, precisely because it is so stupidly dangerous. That makes it remarkable. Worth talking about.

On the other hand, parents are quick to buy double-protective car seats for their seven-year-olds, even if they remember growing up riding without seat belts in Dad's Impala. Going to either extreme is "safer" than staying in the middle.

Edge: Do Less

What you leave out is often worth as much as what you could add. MTV made rock remarkable again (for baby boomers) by leaving out the electricity (their Unplugged program and records sold and sold and sold).

Betty Crocker was unable to convert housewives to cake mixes until they left out the powdered egg from the mix. As soon as the mix did less—you had to add your own egg—women embraced the idea of saving *some* of the hassle of baking. The free prize inside the cake mix was the fact that you still felt like you were being a good housewife, because you did more than just stir up the mix.

Nakednews.com presents the same silly TV-style news as the competition, but the newscasters are, well, wearing less. And the Four Sisters restaurant in Myanmar doesn't bother with a check—you pay what you think the meal is worth. Federal

Express increased customer satisfaction by letting shippers make their own labels, track their own packages and correct their own invoices.

Edge: Treat People Unequally

American Express offers the black Centurion Card, but you can't have one. You can't get into the Groucho Club in England for a drink. And there are nightclubs all over the world that only let in people who are better looking than you and me.

Have you noticed that supermarkets do exactly the wrong thing? They reward their very worst customers (those buying a six-pack and a pack of Kraft Singles) with a supershort line, while the schmo who's buying $300 worth of groceries for a family of four is punished with the very longest line.

What if you reversed it? What if you bent over backward to treat your very best customers *dramatically* better than everyone else. What would happen? You'd annoy some low-profit customers. At the same time, your regular customers would see the advantage of becoming great customers. The people in your organization might fight back, afraid to offend the very customers who treat you with disrespect by buying less. The insightful folks at American Express and American Airlines might disagree.

Edge: Maximize (or Minimize)
External Effects of Purchase and Usage

Giving a portion of your proceeds to charity is a nice thing, but it's actually sort of boring, isn't it? Lots of companies do that (which is good) but we hardly notice it anymore (which is not good). What if your company helped a controversial but worthy (to some folks) cause (like broadening gay rights or promoting drilling in the Arctic National Wildlife Refuge) with each purchase? Or what if you hurt a controversial entity with each purchase—like supporting the recall of the governor or the superintendent of schools?

It gets even more powerful when the purchase has a public face. Every time a Prius drives down the street, the driver is standing up for the Sierra Club.

Edge: Fixing What's Broken

Banks have been around for thousands of years. They're supposed to be big, imposing buildings with limited hours, an imperious staff and no fun. Commerce Bank took a look at that system and decided to start from scratch. They're located in standard retail spaces, they're open seven days a week and they don't have teller windows. They're nice. And they don't charge you to count your pennies.

In response to a string of bank robberies, they responded by doing . . . nothing. They refuse to inconvenience their best customers in order to avoid the rare robbery.

When you identify what's broken among your competitors, you've found a free prize. Being able to bank on Sundays is obviously more important to most New Yorkers than clever billboards or a fancy building.

Edge: Breaking an Industry/Redefining the Value Chain

Every industry is built around a fundamental success. The United Way got big once they figured out how to raise money from payroll deduction. Gillette realized that they could give away razors and make money from blades. Once the fundamental success is established, most organizations surround their profitable cornerstone products with plenty of other activities that don't make very much money—they're used to charging a lot for something that doesn't cost them much, which helps subsidize everything else they do.

If you are willing to go to the edges and change that system, you can win. Schwab did it when they turned the stockbroker fee system upside down. Instead of living off broker's fees and giving everything else away, they did away with a lot of the overhead and then slashed their fees. The competition couldn't respond, because the edge Schwab went to was a place where they couldn't follow.

Arco did it when they started charging extra to accept credit cards. Southwest decided that instead of spending money on bad airline food they would rather give it back to the customer.

Hewlett-Packard makes most of the money in their printer division from toner—the printers are sold cheap to get them yet another toner customer. So what happens when someone shows up and starts selling compatible toner without worrying about subsidizing the cost of the printers?

Edge: Who Sells It

We associate a product with the way we buy it. We subscribe to the newspaper, for example, but not to books. A juicy edge to shoot for is changing the very way the object is sold. The Girl Scouts did this when they moved cookies from the supermarket to your front door. Brownie Wise did the same thing with Tupperware. I succeeded with my books by moving to the Internet as fast as I could.

One of my favorite examples is the March of Dimes. They've captured the attention of millions by tapping into the network in a new way: They fund-raise by putting community leaders in "prison." Now, these local luminaries need to call all their friends to bail them out by soliciting donations to the charity. Not surprisingly, the response rate is huge. March of Dimes has changed its sales force from telemarketers and direct mail to influential community leaders calling their friends.

Or check out Peace Frogs. This successful line of clothing (focused on, not surprisingly, frogs, world peace and quality) is now sold out of refurbished VW vans, parked in high-traffic locations like shopping malls.

If you had to fire your sales force, rejigger your franchises or find a way to sell without a sales force at all, could you?

Edge: Jump the Retail Channel

Cranium is glad they skipped the toy store and decided to sell their board games at Starbucks. Games don't belong at the cash register of a coffee shop, which is exactly why they sold so many copies. Sort of like the candy at Bed Bath & Beyond or a classical music compilation CD at Victoria's Secret (the best-selling classical CD of the year a few years ago, in fact).

Netflix is the poster child for dot-com success stories because they simultaneously eliminated the video store *and* changed the way users think about time when it comes to video rental. By eliminating late fees, they created a huge free prize. Yes, the DVDs are the same, but the way you get them is totally different.

Edge: Convenience (or Not)

Why does wine come with corks? The new artificial corks are, by most measures, easier, more consistent and less fragile. But the free prize you buy when you choose some fancy wine isn't how convenient it is to open the bottle! The rusticity matters. Or consider Johnny's Pizza, the best in Mount Vernon, that's closed on Sundays and won't accept phone orders from strangers.

Lunchables built a billion-dollar business by making lunch

junk into convenient lunch junk. Landfills are groaning because the marketers at Lunchables understood that people would pay a huge premium for little sealed compartments of food.

Can you make your packaging reusable, or much easier (or harder) to use? What about your Web site? Jim Leff keeps the chowhound.com site intentionally clunky. Last month, he got three hundred thousand visitors with no promotion. No, your site won't take off just because you make it difficult to navigate and not so pretty. Taken as a consistent message, though, this nondesign becomes design.

Edge: Sales Method

Jay Walker (of Priceline fame) made his first fortune from New-Sub Services. His edgecraft? Selling magazine subscriptions by subscription! His telemarketers offered an attractive deal to someone willing to use a credit card to buy an endless subscription to *Vogue* or *Gourmet*.

You can also focus on unbundling existing services, selling them one at a time. Like buying reflexology at an airport, instead of having to buy an entire line of services at an official spa.

Edge: Hours of Operation

I'm not sure who buys Korean food at four A.M. at Kang Suh, but it's nice to know that you can. Exactly! The fact that they're open twenty-four hours a day is something that people decide is worth remembering.

Compare this to Jim Leff's discovery of the best barbecue in New York City—which takes place once a year at an annual church fund-raiser. The scarcity of supply means that thousands of people come from miles away because if they don't they'll have to wait a whole year for another shot.

I live near a shoe store that's open only on Wednesdays and Thursdays. What if you do your next grand opening in the middle of the night? Or if you hire actors to read Shakespeare for twenty-four hours without cease? What if you run a sale that lasts only forty-four minutes? Or deliver books bought online the very same day?

Edge: Expectations (Do the Opposite)

I got a nice note from a banker in Texas. She had a limited budget, and she wanted to know how to promote the fact that the bank had more ATMs in the community than the competition. My idea? Without telling anyone, start putting a few $100 bills in the $20 bill storage bin of the ATMs. Not too many, just a few, at random.

Word would spread! By confounding expectations and doing the opposite, you reach an edge. (Alas, this promotion never happened because the woman I gave the idea to didn't know how to become a champion.)

You can make an infants' toy that is completely safe but that looks really dangerous. You could introduce a rock band to your church services. You can make loud things quiet and fat things skinny. You can put lollipops in the bills you send out.

One of the most popular fruits in Asia (durian) smells like baby vomit. Go figure.

Edge: Make It Visible (or Invisible)

One of the secrets of the success of the Dyson vacuum cleaner is that there is no bag. Instead, there's a clear plastic canister. Whenever a friend sees a Dyson in use for the first time, the reaction is always the same—a gasp at how much junk was in that carpet!

On the other hand, when Kellogg's developed Crispix cereal, they closed the tours of their factory (people used to go to Battle Creek to watch them Krispie up the Rice). By turning the creation of a breakfast cereal into a secret, Kellogg's was trying to focus our attention on the product itself by hiding the process. The Canadians did the same thing with the mysterious Caramilk candy bar, which features little pockets of melted caramel inside of milk chocolate.

Edge: Staff Interaction

What if your hotel was staffed with employees empowered to be nasty to demanding guests? One of my favorite resorts keeps a list of people who are banned for life—for treating the place with too little respect. Normally high-maintenance customers know they have to be on good behavior or risk being booted, and it's easy to talk about it.

Compare this to José, who waited on me at a taco shop at the Denver airport. My expectations were close to zero. He confounded them by spending an extra minute chatting with me, getting me a special condiment from the fridge in the back and asking me how my lunch was a minute or two later. Cost: zero. Value: enormous.

Edge: Longevity

You can make your product disposable (cameras, phones, eyeglasses and DVDs are all on this list) or remarkably long lasting (rechargeable batteries and the amazing Silpat reusable parchment baking paper come to mind). Many years ago, my dad had his briefcase stolen. He was sad about the lost papers, cash and ID. But what he missed the most (and still misses) was his lifetime membership card from an airline club.

We have expectations about how long something is supposed to last. When it contradicts those expectations in a dramatic way, it can become remarkable.

Edge: Formalize Your Network

Meetup.com, Jeepfest and comic book conventions are all built around the idea of building a community around a product or service. Meetup organizes monthly get-togethers for millions of people on thousands of topics. By becoming the network, they profit. The opportunity demonstrated by Meetup is to do *just* the fan club (without being the star, the product itself).

Frequent-flier miles go halfway—they reward frequent travelers, but they don't encourage a networking effect (in fact, they do the opposite). If American Airlines had an eBay-like service where people could buy and sell and swap their miles, miles would become worth more.

Edge: Make Fun of It

Why is business (and philanthropy and education for that matter) so serious? The Sierra Club discovered that putting up a parody site about a giant new SUV (the Humdinger) was a great way to attract attention. Archie McPhee continues to thrive by making fun of nuns, albino bowlers, rabbis and monkeys.

> What would Bozo do?

Why do most airlines insist on using mumbo jumbo when they talk to us (like the word "pre-board") and pretend that everything they do is so serious? Instead of yelling about which rows should get on the plane first, why not paste footprints on the floor of the terminal, and ask everyone to stand on the footprint that matches their row number?

Of course, you can also make a silly thing serious. Rice to Riches is a successful chain-to-be, selling very serious rice pudding at very serious prices. You can also buy a $120 Samurai

Yo-yo, the best ever made, and it's very much not a toy—it's a sporting good, a tool for a professional.

Edge: Get an Expert to Switch Fields
Michael Graves designs teapots and storage sheds. George Foreman sells grills and celebrity chef Anthony Bourdain writes novels, as does professional wrestler Mick Foley. If any unrelated expert could change your product or service, who would it be? What would they do?

Edge: Move
When Apple started putting computer stores in upscale malls, people said they were crazy. The rent is too high to make it pay. Not so. More than half the people walking into an Apple store don't own one (yet). Apple has found a great way to tell its story to new prospects. By being remarkable in the juxtaposition of the product and the place, they got the attention of people who would never drive out of their way to go to one (and yes, the stores are incredibly profitable).

Walking in the mall with a friend, it's hard to comment on yet another shoe store. But when you've got the chance to take a break from soft goods and play with the latest Apple toys . . . that's something to talk about. At the same time that Apple is putting an unusual retail store in a mall, others are putting retail outlets in museums or on airplanes or putting restaurants in furniture stores—all tactics that can make people sit up and notice.

Enterprise Rent-A-Car has done quite well by abandoning the airport. By being the only major car rental brand in your neighborhood, they become the first and only choice if you've had an accident or your car is in the shop.

Edge: Media

Everyone with an interesting story to tell wants to be in the media. And they usually fail, because the story isn't *that* interesting and the media is awfully difficult to rouse to a new idea.

A few companies have followed the remarkable path of refusing to talk to the press. Segway's huge media bonanza came as a direct result of their secrecy. BzzAgent continues its rapid growth at the same time it warns the press on their Web site to please not write about them.

The flip side of this approach is to live your life in public. Joi Ito does this with his blog. The Spice Girls were famous mostly because they were famous. What if your company posted all its internal documents? Linux continues to grow by being totally transparent. Why not you?

Case Study: How Master Lock Improved Sales 50 Percent

Using free-prize thinking (and a focus on design), Master Lock redesigned their core product line. By changing both the padlock and the box, they reinvented the business.

Their first insight was understanding that people try to buy locks in the section of the store where the thing that they want to lock up is sold. So bike locks need to be near bikes, while locker locks need to be near school supplies. By clearly labeling each lock for its special function, Master Lock made it easier for the purchasers to feel comfortable with their choice—even if all the locks are pretty similar.

Second, they made the lock easier to use. They put the keyhole in the front, instead of on the bottom. A design decision, like the box.

And finally, they added a colored rubber bumper, and keys that matched the color of the bumper, making it easier to find the right key for the lock you're trying to open.

Four simple design changes: a smarter box, better key placement, no-scratch bumpers and color-coded keys.

None of these things increases the security of the lock, of course. All of them dramatically increase its functionality, which led to a boom in sales.

When to Cut Bait: It's Not About You

I want to share the story of Specialty Films & Associates for two reasons. First, because they're a classic business-to-business business, reinforcing my point that all of these ideas can apply precisely to industrial suppliers as well as any other business. Second, they did the thing almost no one is willing to do. They quit and started over.

Tony Cherot and Jane Dirr started Specialty Films & Associates as the purest sort of business-to-business venture. Their idea? To act as a middleman between packaged goods companies (like bakeries) and factories that made commodity-packaging products (e.g., three-sided seal bags for chips and cookies, medical fluid pouches and film laminates). It's easy to imagine that in the hardheaded world of packaged goods, smart buyers would do anything to save a penny or two on packaging, and the way Tony and Jane would win would be through aggressive procurement and smart salesmanship. They were classic middlemen.

Most of the time, people in this situation are looking for marketing to serve as a magic elixir. They want to know how to use marketing techniques to make the business they've chosen work more profitably with the customers they're targeting. They want to charge better-than-commodity prices for their commodity products. They usually believe that it is the job of marketing to focus the spotlight on the things they've already decided to sell.

Fortunately for Tony and Jane, they saw beyond that. They realized that everything they do is marketing, and that included their choice of product line. Rather than arguing with the market, they cut bait. They changed their business.

"By closely studying the operations of the converters who supplied us, we saw inefficiencies in lead times, raw materials procurement, printing capabilities and responsiveness to the customer," said Cherot. They decided to *become* the factory, and to create only remarkable products. They bought the machines and figured out how to use them better, to use them in a re-markable way that no one else could.

By inventing new ways for companies to use packaging, they reinvented their entire industry. Once again, the product be-came the marketing. It isn't their Web site or brochure that's re-markable, it's the supercool pouches, zipper closures, film laminates and stuff that they make for companies like Keebler and others. By combining insanely fast turnaround with cutting-edge products, they've discovered that the marketing takes care of itself.

Case Study: Flashlight Thinking (and a Bonus)

If you don't settle for differentiation, you can explore the edges in almost any industry. Consider flashlights. It started with a quest to make lights that felt significantly more powerful (con-sider the Maglite police flashlights, which weigh several pounds each and make anyone feel like a night watchman).

Then Freeplay introduced a light that wasn't just efficient, it used *no* batteries whatsoever.

This was followed by the $200 SureFire M6, which is half the size but thirty times brighter than a standard flashlight. It's im-possible to use one without having a conversation, even if it's only with a nearby bear or a squirrel.

While I'm talking about flashlights, let me also talk about showers. In hotels.

No one picks a hotel by the shower, right?

Well, the Serrano in San Francisco (a Kimpton hotel) has a shower that, according to author Jackie Huba, "was huge, probably ten feet by fourteen feet, had a stereo system with speakers, had a shower with eight—eight—shower heads, including an overhead waterfall and had TV in the shower, with speakers." You can find a photo link in the endnotes.

Too fancy? The Starwood chain has started doing a $15 modification to the showers in its fancier hotels (like the St. Regis). Using a bent shower rod instead of a straight one, they avoid the sticky Holiday Inn billow, in which the rushing water of the shower causes the shower curtain to blow into the shower, making you feel trapped.

Still too big an investment? How about this insight I came up with at the St. Regis in Aspen (which apparently hasn't gotten the curved shower rods yet). The shower curtains at this very expensive hotel were cheap and charmless. What if the management played on the celebrity obsession of the town and handed any celebrity who stayed over a Sharpie marker and asked him to autograph the inside of the shower curtain in big black letters? I don't know about you, but if I saw Gwyneth's or Mick's autograph inside my shower, I'd mention it, say, five hundred times.

A Nine-Year-Old Kid Can Do Edgecraft

While the edges always change, the process never does. Here's how you do it:

1. Find a product or service that's completely unrelated to your industry.

2. Figure out who's winning by being remarkable.

3. Discover which edge they went to.

4. Do that in your own industry.

Crest figured out how to make money with remarkably cheap electric toothbrushes. What if companies like Gillette or Henckels or Oster or Braun or Playtex or Toro or Sony decided to go to the same edge?

Don't copy the specific tactics. Figure out how you can get to the very same edge but in a different way. If a restaurant captured the attention of its audience by offering an all-you-can-eat chili pepper night, that doesn't mean that your hardware store should start selling chili peppers. Instead, realize that people are attracted to excess. You can offer the contractors in town all the bricks they can carry to their truck for $9 instead. And post the name of the guy who carried the most on a sign by the cash register. (And why not list the guy who carried the least while you're at it?)

Philadelphia is home to the original manufacturer of push-pins (for bulletin boards). More than a hundred years old, they're getting killed by cheap imports. The solution? Go to the edge used by T-shirt manufacturers. Make a bigger pushpin and start putting words and phrases on each pin. Start with easy things like "critical path" or "nice work" and then move up to li-censed phrases and images. It transforms an invisible item into a visible one, the same way an imprinted T-shirt does. No one would consider spending $25 for a plain white Hanes T-shirt. Add a silk-screen logo and that high-profit sale happens every day at rock concerts and Disney World.

Or consider the lawn care company that realized that in a world of one-click Internet buying, waiting two weeks for a quote on lawn care was just too long. Using a combination of satellite photos and tax records, they're able to quote a home-owner a cost for service *before* they're even contacted. Now, whenever they go out to treat a customer's lawn, the driver brings a stack of Frisbees with him. Each Frisbee has a prospect's address and price quote printed on a sticker affixed to it. As the driver drives down the street to the job, he tosses the Frisbee onto the neighbor's lawn. By radically changing the time frame (from two weeks to one minute) they offer con-sumers a free prize.

It's about being remarkable to people who sneeze!*

Nine People Who Went to the Edges

Before the endnotes, I thought I'd leave you with some examples that really attracted my attention. I have no idea if these tactics will work for you—they probably won't, in fact—but once you get in the habit of noticing things like this, it'll make it easier for you to find your own edge.

1. The front door at Hotel Unique in São Paolo, Brazil, is twenty-five feet high and weighs 650 pounds. No one stays in a hotel because of the front door, yet this is one of the reasons why this hotel stands out from the other thirty thousand in town (the astounding architecture is part of it as well). Soon after opening, the place was totally jammed, all because of the free prize that style and flair deliver.

2. Joi Ito's Web site is one of the most popular blogs in the world. Why? Joi has decided to live his life online. He's constantly sharing his thoughts, his opportunities, and his

---

*A sneezer is someone of influence in the community (whatever community) that spreads the word about a product or service. When an idea gets sneezed, it spreads and, ultimately, if you're lucky, becomes an ideavirus. You can read all about this in my book *Unleashing the Ideavirus*, which is in bookstores or free on the Internet.

Rolodex with the rest of the world. By eliminating the barriers of privacy, he delivers more than the average blog—and people respond to it (you can even be posted on his site—all you have to do is send him your birthday).

3. Ringtones are the silliest multimillion-dollar business I can think of. Thomas Dolby (of "She Blinded Me with Science" fame) is poised to make a killing with his www.retroringtones.com ringtone wholesaling business. Here's my bet: After you hear a few of his samples, you'll do what I did, which is trade in your old cell phone for no other reason than to have Richard Nixon or Jimi Hendrix announce your calls. This is classic free-prize thinking.

4. Niman Ranch will sell you four hormone-free, antibiotic-free, humanely raised beef-based hot dogs for about $7. Possibly the finest hot dogs in the world. It's not clear that the average kid eating a wiener can taste the difference, which is my whole point ... the way we feel about what we eat counts for as much as the taste itself.

5. On the topic of hot dogs, consider PacBell Stadium in San Francisco. While the Giants might not have made the World Series this year, going to the game is far more appealing now that they serve the best food in the major leagues (they even serve freshly made sushi).

   Sushi at a ball game? Not for everyone, which makes it even more remarkable. George Steinbrenner wants to build a new stadium for the Yankees. Perhaps he should start by getting a world-class concession service (and a new PA system while he's at it). A ball game is about more than watching the Yankees play. You can do that at home.

6. Ann Sacks (tile) and Waterworks (bath and kitchen fixtures) both started out with a simple edge: sell less. Rather than offering a complete line of products that covered all price ranges, they sought out the exclusive, the unusual and the remarkable.

7. In the early 1970s, the Boston Consulting Group burst into the limelight by naming the "BCG growth-share matrix." This fancy analysis is actually pretty obvious, but by naming it and turning it into a tool, they propelled themselves into the top tier of high-priced consulting firms. I have no idea if their advice is better, but it's easier to talk about.

8. Back in the day, when installing a computer network was really and truly difficult, Novell (the leader at the time) started certifying consultants in their technology. Of course, companies were buying a network, not certification, but the peace of mind became the free prize.

9. When Susan Beattie helped start T. Lloyd Clothiers (in Portsmouth, NH) in May 2002, she had a tough row to hoe. This is an upscale retail apparel store carrying brands with snob appeal. From the first day, she decided to build a store that would appeal to *her* if she was a customer. She was sick of being treated with disdain or indifference at many of the

stores she visited—so she was determined to always offer customers respect, caring, connection and community. Not a little—a lot. They went all the way to the edge.

Less than a year later, in an economy bereft of leadership or optimism, they are getting ready to double in size by opening their second store on Boston's North Shore. The process of buying the clothes is obviously as important to customers as the clothes themselves.

Marketing Is Dead. Long Live Marketing

At my seminars, I like to spend the last two hours riffing with the audience. People discuss what they do and we talk about how their organizations can grow when their competitors don't.

What I've seen again and again is this: People want marketing to solve their product problems.

One participant talked with enthusiasm about his business making tiny CD-ROM business cards. You may have seen these—they're about the size of a deck of cards, and they can contain a little video or a link to a Web site or even a computer game. The idea is that an individual or organization would use this as a dramatically enhanced calling card. This entrepreneur liked the idea of replacing the business card (actually, he loved the idea), but his sales were disappointing.

The problem is that CD-ROM business cards have been

around for a while and they're not taking off. People are aware of them, but they don't seem to want one. This manager, like most managers, doesn't want to give up.

Rather than arguing with the market—fighting to market this commodity product in a better way—I encouraged this entrepreneur to change his *product,* not the marketing. Instead of selling CD-ROM business cards, why not sell CD-ROM tours of houses for sale (that people can post on community bulletin boards, say) or CD-ROM head shots of actors, or . . .

By redefining the way he used and talked about this device, he could reinvent himself and his industry. He could find a marketplace that was just as viral but more responsive to the idea itself.

The marketing imperative has shifted. We now live in a world where it's all marketing, where the game changes faster than ever and where you often get only one shot at making things work. That means that we need to take a hard look at what we make, how we make it and to whom we sell it.

None of this is hard. It's all difficult. It takes a commitment to do something that matters. So go . . . make something happen!

FIVE QUESTIONS

1. If we knew the right answer, would that be enough to solve our problem?

2. Which edges are working for unrelated organizations?

3. Could we get closer to the edge?

4. How do we make our product or service public, not private?

5. Is it *really* remarkable?

NOTES

x   *Yes,* there are a lot of endnotes. Some of them are merely pointers to interesting references online. Others are very long, detailed explanations of stuff I talked about in the book. I've found in previous books that some people want the big picture and others want every detail. I thought this might be a neat way to do both. Even better, the notes have been updated since this book was printed, which means you can get a whole new set for free by visiting http://www.freeprizeinside.com. Thanks.

1   **My partner:** Here I talked about my old business partner. Steve turned his knack for practical insight into a career that went from Harvard Business School to the senior executive suite at Sears. I can sure pick 'em sometimes.

5   **Amazon reported:** *New York Times,* September 23, 2003, p. C4.

6   **"This campaign really":** Ibid., p. C8.

6   **Sixty million dollars:** Does Yahoo! really need to spend $40 million on advertising?

8   **If marketing is about:** Before you can communicate that you've

solved the problem, it helps to understand what the problem is. And more often than not, the consumer doesn't know.

10 **You can innovate:** I talk about the fact that incremental improvement isn't powerful enough to get people to switch to your product in droves. Many people don't want this to be true. They don't want to have innovation be the only path to growth. They believe that the market should reward earnest efforts at incremental improvement. Alas, it doesn't matter what you want . . . what we see is that the market rewards innovation.

10 **more than half the buyers:** The Lincoln-Mercury story has many variations. The Diamond Jubilee edition, made in 1978, is probably the most egregious—the option package cost more than most cars.

11 **The simple fact is:** The reason the curve is not straight is that ever-increasing investments require higher cost of capital, higher overhead and more risk amelioration. As a result, the return from a huge investment has to be higher (on a percentage basis) because otherwise the investors would prefer to make diversified bets in small projects.

12 **When Iridium invested:** http://www.wired.com/news/business/0,1367,19920,00.html

12 **how much revenue you can:** I'll admit that the curve on page 12 is a bit more controversial, but if you think about it, it makes sense. Think about the race to build the world's fastest supercomputer a few years ago. Fujitsu spent hundreds of millions of dol-

lars on it. Or the Taligent debacle, which involved investments of a similar scale from IBM and others.

One of the biggest lessons of the dot-com flame-outs was that spending $100 million or more in TV advertising had little effect on actually building a business or a brand. While the commercials may have been entertaining, the return on investment wasn't there.

So, what we see is that the closer we get to the right or left side of the curve, the *lower* the return on investment actually turns out to be. You may have to make fewer decisions (big bets take as much decision time as smaller ones) but you pay for the privilege.

15 **Each incremental dollar:** I point out that the payoff from technology is decreasing. One of the big reasons for this is that the amount of technology is skyrocketing. In 1900, roughly 25,000 patents were issued. By 1950 that number had jumped modestly to 43,000. But since 1950 there has been a tripling of the number of patents to nearly 150,000 awarded every year since 1997. Having a cool gizmo isn't enough when there are millions of cool gizmos to choose from.

15 **Consumers (at home):** Throughout this book (and every book I write, in fact) whenever I say "consumer," I really mean someone who buys things, whether it's at home or at work. An ad buyer or a

conveyor belt purchasing agent are both consumers, as far as I'm concerned. Organizations don't decide to buy stuff . . . people do.

15 **We want cool stuff:** Not sure you buy the validity of the idea about want and need on page 15? Take the *Consumer Reports* reality-check test. Read a review in *CR* of a category you know a lot about. See if you agree with their findings. See if you bought the product they recommend. If you're like most people I know, the answer is no.

16 **at record levels:** http://www.jdpower.com/presspass/pr/images/2003058afull.gif

16 **people are buying the car:** I touch on branding a bit on page 15. Jim Leff is one of the great food writers of our time. Here's something he wrote about branding in a recent newsletter: "Over the past century, marketers have learned to psychologically manipulate consumers into buying not on the basis of quality but in response to the specialized form of hypnosis known as branding. The human psyche has been hacked to the point where masses can be persuaded to gladly embrace poor-value, low-quality products. The plethora of choices has shriveled, value declines as prices rise, and any number of realms are getting worse, not better.

"Most consumers have not only stopped demanding quality, but quality has, in many cases, become entirely irrelevant. For example, millions have an emotional bond with Budweiser that has nothing whatever to do with its flavor."

Of course, Jim is right that Budweiser is not a great beverage. But it is certainly true that it's a great beer, if you define beer as a beverage that makes you feel powerful and sexy and part of a clan when you drink it! The brand (built at a cost of more than $1 billion), which you surely can't afford to replicate, is very much part of what you buy when you buy the product.

Jim continues a bit later, "They buy Bud because of how the brand (not the actual product) makes them feel about themselves. It's about everything but beer. The preference of Bud loyalists stems from the insidious power of post-hypnotic suggestion continuously reinforced through keenly targeted marketing."

When you go to a fancy restaurant, are you buying the food or the chef? Jim sees it this way: "The upper-level assault, which is just starting to reveal itself, seems to involve spinning brand webs around hyped star chefs, using their premium images to assure upscale patrons of meals of sufficiently high prestige (most high-end spots—including the genuinely terrific ones—are patronized for their prestige). Figures like Bobby Flay and Emeril are the latter-day upscale analogs of Ronald McDonald. . . ."

Jim may not like it ("Understand, please, that I'm not anti-corporate. I'm just anti-sucking.") but the fact is, people seem to *like* the nondescript food as long as the free prize (the famous chef) is included. My personal feelings lie with my fellow chowhound Jim, but, alas, it's clear that as in all things, the market prefers the prize to the main attraction.

Before I let my friend Jim go, I want to share two more paragraphs he wrote on Panera Bread, which was the proximate cause of this rant:

"But no. The pineapple upside down tart—like everything I've tried from Panera—was horrid. It wasn't just tasteless and mediocre and wrong and offensive. It created rippling spiritual and physical aftershocks. Eating it left me feeling deeply vacant, the way a burger and fries at McDonald's does (only worse, because one steels oneself for the 'great taste' of McDonald's). And it upset my stomach. My mother—who has infallible taste in baked goods—proclaimed it, with a look of sour and confused displeasure, as 'gooey.'

"Panera's products are remarkable, though, in that they've developed an entirely new style of sucking. Their products don't suck in any of the usual ways; they're a fresh take on suckiness built from scratch. Since nothing sucks familiarly, Panera's stuff can fool you at first if you don't pay close attention."

The problem, of course, doesn't lie with *all* marketers. It's marketers who don't bother to make truly great stuff at the same time that they build the facade that makes people *expect* good stuff. The incremental cost of making a truly great pineapple upside-down cake (like the incremental cost of Starbucks making great coffee) is tiny. What separates a product that grows for the ages from one that just grows and crashes is the ability to appeal to both worlds—the folks that want the fortune *and* the ones who want the cookie.

16   **selling T-shirts:** http://www.totalrecall2003.com/index.htm

17   **a profitable venture:** I riff on the high payoff of design. It's free. Free as in your revenue minus your costs is zero or more. Yes, you need to pay for great design. No, it doesn't cost you anything.

21   **one endless, mind-numbing strip:** As you can guess, I've driven the road described here more than a few times. My favorite part? If you keep going you'll see, off in the distance, almost like a mirage, a steel bridge (painted orange) spanning the highway. The bridge is for pedestrians only, and it was built with private funds. Weber's, Canada's most famous hamburger stand, built the bridge so that southbound motorists with a craving for one of their hamburgers

wouldn't have to risk their lives crossing the highway to get to this tiny (but very busy) hamburger stand. A combination of great location—halfway to where you're going!—and a remarkable burger turned Weber's into an institution.

But I don't want to tell you about Paul Weber's burgers. I want to talk about his neighbor, Rita Robinson. Rita runs a store in a little strip mall that's had more than its fair share of tenants.

Everyone thinks that being one hundred meters away from Weber's is the ticket to success, but the businesses come, and, just as quickly, go. Rita's store is different.

23 **you're spending so much time:** Another Apple thought for you: Did you notice that the way their products look has a lot to do with the loyalty inspired in their users? Take a look at http://www.billnoll.com/g5/ and you'll see the beauty designed into the G5. It's easy to argue that a computer should run fast and not crash and be cheap, period. But Apple's survival (and the leverage they've got) belie this point.

23 **the chain of:** Ramit Sethi interviewed Ann Willoughby.

24 **Dr. Peter Pronovost:** Dr. Pronovost was interviewed by Ramit Sethi. When he invented the checklist, he was a standard ICU doctor, nothing fancy. Since then, he's been promoted to medical director of the Center for Innovations in Quality Patient Care at Johns Hopkins.

24 **They're buying:** Sure it cost Apple money to write the software that syncs the music with your computer. Sure the mold for the iPod wasn't cheap. But these innovations—the idea of sync and the sketch of the iPod that Jonathan Ivey at Apple did—were about insight, not cash.

25   **haircuts:** *Wall Street Journal*, September 22, 2003.

26   ***The New York Times:*** *The New York Times* talked about the price of
wow in an article about high-priced New York real estate (apparently, $10 million doesn't buy much anymore).

31   **which would you choose?:** In talking about gimmicks, I talked about
American Express. When I was running Yoyodyne, the online pro-
motions company, we devised a wintertime sweepstakes designed to
reward people for shopping online. We gave away $1 million in
prizes to entice consumers to get involved. American Express loved
the idea and sponsored it. Visa thought it was a gimmick, something
that would tarnish their brand. They ended up spending twenty
times as much as we were asking them for—they sponsored a portal
instead. American Express ended up with a huge return on investment. Which was the gimmick?

31   **A gimmick?:** Thanks to Alex Godin for researching the Wrigley gum
story.

33   **They sold the company:** It's worth a note here that many high-flying
companies ended up getting severely punished for what really *was* a
gimmick. The accounting maneuvers that delivered the numbers
that Wall Street said they wanted marked the end of their bull run.
Clearly, lying about their financial status *wasn't* something that the
investors were hoping for. It was a gimmick, through and through.

34   **the zip code:** Actually, according to Postal Service officials, Robert
Moon only invented the first three digits of the zip code. Someone
else, identity unknown, contributed the next two. I kid you not.

35   **dozens of clubs:** On health clubs: My wife likes to tell the story of the

woman who used to work out at her gym—in her office clothes. After an hour on the treadmill, she'd wipe off her face, change her shoes and head back to work, blissfully unaware of the locker room.

35   **An original Picasso:** Yes, the Picasso at the Four Seasons was expensive. But the tens of thousands of $27 chickens that painting has sold have more than paid for it.

> 36 **It doesn't matter:** "Far more creativity, today, goes into the marketing of products than into the products themselves."
> —Hubertus Bigend, Founder, Blue Ant

41   **Because your competition:** Not only the guys down the street, but the jerk in the cubicle next to you who's angling to get the promotion you know you deserve.

43   **could walk into Ford's:** I'm defining productivity as the amount of work produced by a given unit of labor. The combination of machines, jigs, assembly lines and repetitive work meant that a strong, motivated worker could dramatically increase his output merely by walking into Ford's plant. Same worker, different output. Productivity has been increasing relentlessly ever since, largely because we've mechanized more and more operations (in both service and product businesses) allowing nongifted individuals to create ever more value.

Computers only accelerated this effort. Now, one worker can cut extraordinarily accurate parts out of sheets of steel using a laser. Telemarketers use predictive dialing to reach the next house on the list without waiting for the phone to ring. The time it takes to create a new Ford car (including the engine) is now less than forty hours of labor, thanks to robots and computer-controlled devices. (http:// lang.motorway.com/home/articles/gmpassford.asp).

Credit card marketers use data mining to separate the likely buyers from the rest of the pack. The reason is that productivity increases are the only way to improve profits without raising prices or cutting the cost of materials.

43   **based on productivity:** Actually, the $5 day wasn't Ford's idea. The idea came from his senior adviser, James Couzens, who later became a U.S. senator. Couzens was reading a socialist magazine (not that there's anything wrong with that) and became incensed over the response to a letter to the editor. The reader wanted to know why the magazine wasn't paying its workers more. The editor's whiny response offended Couzens. "That was an asinine answer!" he later wrote.

Couzens pitched Ford the idea of showing the world a different way of treating labor, and in a few weeks, the deed was done. Douglas Brinkley's history of Ford, *Wheels for the World*, is filled with fascinating examples of good (and bad) championing.

43   **It meant that nearly:** This is true if you define "overpaid" to mean getting paid more than the company could pay someone else to do the same work.

44 **we got used to being paid:** This is even though our output was high through no fault of our own. It was high because the machines in the factory made it high. Better machines could lead to more output, and even though the workers didn't pay for those machines, they came to expect higher pay. The most ridiculous example of this thinking at work is the stupidly high salaries paid to ordinary, non-founding CEOs. These guys get paid a fortune because the very expensive organization they run is making a profit. No thought at all is given to how little it would cost to replace this person with someone as good (or better).

44 **This is why we're insecure:** This explains why jobs are moving to China so fast. Every once in a while, a CEO realizes how much extra she's paying people to do fairly straightforward work that could be easily done on another continent for 5 percent of what she's paying now. Sooner or later, the logic of Henry Ford's largesse breaks down and executives replace the workers who begged to have their jobs automated—with machines or with other people.

I'm fascinated by the analysis of the productivity trap, so let me elaborate on it a bit here. If we take a look at the plot of increased productivity among American workers, it looks a lot like increased pay over time.

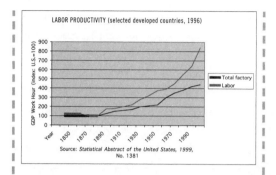

Source: *Statistical Abstract of the United States, 1999,*
No. 1381

Salaries keep rising, but for a lot of workers, the work we do is actually *easier.* Computer-aided telemarketing, computer-aided customer service, computer-aided manufacturing, even computer-aided marketing mean that we're busy following rules that someone else dreamed up.

As a result, many people have gotten their wish—they have boring jobs and they get paid a lot. Agents of change who are agitating for more exciting (and challenging) work are often met with a rolling of the eyes—why on earth would someone want to screw up such a great gig?

The reason is simple. As the gap between replacement cost (how much it would cost the company to outsource your job) and pay based on productivity rises, lots and lots of jobs are going to go overseas or

> get done by a computer. The only option, it seems to
> me, is to make our jobs so engaging, creative, ever
> changing and unpredictable that we're actually *earn-*
> *ing* all that money.

49 **In 2002, Microsoft:** http://www.informationweek.com/story/
IWK20010726S0016

50 **Without a champion:** Cisco had a great strategy for growth. They
knew that champions are hard to grow, so they bought them. Most
high-tech firms are run by someone who championed an idea from
the beginning and built it. When Cisco built an environment that re-
spected and empowered these people, buying their companies became good for both sides. Now the company is filled with people
who understand how to make things happen—it's up to management to get out of their way.

53 **Nouriche, yogurt:** As long as we're talking about food packaging,
consider this December 2002 study from Information Resources, reported in *The New York Times*: Researchers wanted to know what
would get consumers to try a new snack or food. Here are the top six
benefits:

Ready to eat

Heat and eat

On the go

No utensils required

Low carb

Low fat

Amazingly, "tastes good" didn't make the list, and "nutritious" didn't either. Clearly, when it comes to something important, the free prize dominates more needs-based concerns.

57 **you get the memo:** The first edition of this book came in a cereal box. Why? I was trying to make a point about soft innovation, but I was also creating a living, breathing experiment in using the fulcrum and in being a champion.

This time, I knew that I had all three elements in place. I could demonstrate (because I had done *Purple Cow* in a milk carton) that I was the guy to do the project. I knew (for the same reason) that the cereal box was likely to work. And I hoped I could demonstrate that the exercise of putting the book in a box was worth the effort.

So, with the fulcrum in place, is it easy to champion the project? Can a best-selling author command a publisher to do something they've never done before? Here's how the process went—a living example of the fulcrum in action.

I pitched the idea to my publisher. He seemed to like it.

Then I got the memo from someone on his team.

Here's a table from the note:

	Entire first printing with cereal box, followed by normal book, both $19.95.	Simultaneous book and cereal box, retailer's choice, both $19.95.	Slipcover-style small box for the whole first printing—clerks remove slipcover to scan at retail. No shrink wrap.	Only way to get cereal box is via 10-pack, with or without COW or 99COWS.
Can we do a single ISBN to concentrate best-seller impact?	*No: Our warehouse and all systems need to track them as different items.*	*No: Our warehouse and all systems need to track them as different items.*	*Yes*	*No—in fact you need 3 ISBNs so that a store can sell individual cereal boxes.*
Buzz value of the cereal box?	*High*	*Medium*	*Medium*	*Medium*
Sales department concerns?	*Sell-in will be MUCH lower than normal.* *We will have to pay for extra coop at EVERY major account.*	*We will have to pay for extra coop, but only for select accounts.*	*Negative impact on sell-in will depend on size of slipcover—smaller is better.* *Not sure yet about impact on coop.*	*We will have to pay for extra coop, but only for select accounts.*

Warehouse/ Shipping / Returns concerns?	Risk of damaged cereal boxes if we ship partial cartons. Returns will be harder and more expensive to process.	Risk of damaged cereal boxes if we ship partial cartons. Returns will be harder and more expensive to process.	Risk of damaged cereal boxes if we ship partial cartons. Returns will be harder and more expensive to process.	No partial cartons —good thing. Returns will be harder and more expensive to process.
Can we track sales of different versions?	Yes	Yes	No	Yes
Extra production & labor expense?	TK	TK	TK	TK

You can't argue with this table. It's thoughtful, rational and clearly laid out. It's nothing personal—it makes it clear that this is an idea that's just not worth doing.

Of course, I *did* argue with it. Bit by bit, we teased out what the real objections were, what was really hard about putting a book in a box, and then I asked obligating questions. "If we can solve *this* problem, will you be able to support the project?" By digging deeper and deeper, we identified the real problems and stamped them out.

So, you're not the only one who's gotten the memo. It'll happen. And if you really believe in your innovation, you can work with your team to figure out what the hurdles are and address them.

While we're talking about memos, I wanted to take a second to talk about this next memo. This is the one you'll see from the hardworking guy in (insert department here) who is grudgingly going along with your idea, but is still afraid because he sees too much risk. Here's the first memo that my publisher wanted to send to the sales force (I edited it down to a few relevant paragraphs):

WHAT IS THIS THING?

A real cereal box, illustrated in 4-color, with the book inside. Based on the very successful milk carton that Godin self-published for the first edition of *Purple Cow*. It will reclose with a tab so that it looks good even after you break the seal. People will leave it sitting around as a conversation piece. It will help drive buzz and reinforce the message of the book.

HOW BIG WILL IT BE?

The size of a Grape Nuts box—dimensions TK. Not that much bigger than a fat hardcover.

DOES IT COST MORE THAN THE REGULAR BOOK?

No—both versions will have a $19.95 cover price.

DO RETAILERS HAVE TO TAKE THE BOOK IN A CEREAL BOX?

No—we will offer every account a choice to order books with or without the cereal box. We believe the cereal box version will sell better on a display table, but we understand that not every retailer is *willing to take that risk* [all italics are mine].

The catch is that if you want to sell the cereal boxes, you have to order in multiples of 10—we will only be shipping them in prepacks of 10.

Seth believes that the biggest demand will come from Amazon, bn.com, and 800-CEO-READ. Seth will be promoting it to his mailing list of about 10,000 hardcore fans, and those people tend to buy online. They cleaned him out of about 9,000 *Purple Cow* milk cartons in 19 days, after his excerpt ran in *Fast Company*.

WON'T CEREAL BOXES GET
EASILY DAMAGED DURING SHIPPING?

Since they will ONLY come in 10-packs, that eliminates the problem of mixed ships that might damage the boxes.

We do need to make sure the 10-packs are sturdy enough to be stacked up very high without damaging the cereal boxes. This might require special cardboard—details TK.

WON'T THE CEREAL BOX VERSION HAVE TO HAVE A SEPARATE ISBN? AND WON'T THAT SCREW UP BEST-SELLER REPORTING?

The cereal box itself will have a phantom ISBN for SAP tracking only. However, it *won't* have a bar code matching that ISBN. Instead, it will have the *exact same bar code as the book itself,* so that it will scan at cash registers the exact same way as the plain hardcover, for joint best-seller tracking.

The key to making this work is that the warehouse will NEVER handle the cereal box as an independent object. They will receive finished prepacks from the outside vendor—the vendor will have to put the books into the cereal boxes and then the cereal boxes into the prepacks.

The catalog (and the warehouse) will only deal with two ISBNs—one for the plain hardcover, one for the 10-pack of cereal boxes.

The big drawback to this single ISBN is that if (for example) B&N orders 4000 cereal boxes and 4000 loose hardcovers, we'll have no way of knowing which edition is selling better, since they will scan exactly the same way. But it seems worth it to try to get on some best-seller lists.

How Many Cereal Boxes Are We Going to Print?

Hard to predict yet—maybe 5k, maybe 10k, maybe a lot more. Seth thinks the biggest demand will come from Amazon, BN.com, and 800-CEO-READ.

Fortunately, before the publisher spread gloom too far, they asked me to take a look. Here's my revised memo:

HOW A MILK CARTON CREATED
A *NEW YORK TIMES* BEST SELLER

Seth Godin's previous book *Purple Cow* hit #8 on the *Times* hardcover how-to list. There are a lot of reasons, but a big one was the nearly instant sale of the first 10,000 copies.

All 10,000 copies came inside a real milk carton. They were snapped up in 19 days, entirely online. This led to a great deal of buzz and a very warm reception for the hardcover edition.

Godin is back with an even better idea. His new book, *Free Prize Inside,* comes inside a real cereal box, illustrated in 4-color, with the book inside. It will reclose with a tab so that it looks good even after you break the seal. People will leave it sitting around as a conversation piece. More important, it makes it easier to give the book to a colleague—they don't call it a conversation piece for nothing. It will help drive buzz and reinforce the message of the book.

Instead of just offering this special packaging online, we've prevailed on the author to make it available to any retailer that wants it—but there's a catch.

WHAT'S THE CATCH?

Even though the specially packaged book costs *exactly the same* as the book without the package, we're only committed to producing it for the first print run. Accounts that fail to order the special packaging in advance can't get it.

The box is not much bigger than a big hardcover, and there's no requirement for the retailer to keep the box if they decide (whenever) that it's easier to shelve without it.

DOES IT COST MORE THAN THE REGULAR BOOK?

No—both versions will have a $19.95 cover price.

DO RETAILERS HAVE TO TAKE THE BOOK IN A CEREAL BOX?

No—we will offer every account a choice to order books with or without the cereal box. We believe the cereal box version will sell better on a display table, but we understand that some retailers will insist on business as usual. (Please don't have them yell at us if they fail to order enough at the start!)

Books without the box can be ordered in ones and twos, but in order to get cereal boxes, you have to order in multiples of 10—we will only be shipping them in prepacks.

Any retailer that wants to be included on Seth's Web site (the center of the huge online promotion that is his trademark) will be included at no charge if they order the prepacks.

WON'T CEREAL BOXES GET
EASILY DAMAGED DURING SHIPPING?

Hey, cereal boxes in the supermarket don't get damaged! We'll be shipping the prepacks in a secure way so there will be no damage.

WON'T THE CEREAL BOX VERSION HAVE TO HAVE A SEPARATE
ISBN? AND WON'T THAT SCREW UP BEST-SELLER REPORTING?

Glad you asked! The cereal box itself will have a phantom ISBN for SAP tracking only. However, it *won't* have a bar code matching the SAP number. Instead, it will have the *exact same bar code as the book itself,* so that it will scan at cash registers the same way as the plain hardcover. The book is the book, and we'll get the same best-seller credit regardless of whether the box is used or not.

(Not that you asked, but our warehouse will never need to handle the cereal box as an independent object. They will receive finished prepacks from the outside cereal box vendor—the vendor will put the books into the cereal boxes and then the cereal boxes into the prepacks—no hassle for us, for you or for the retailer.)

The catalog (and the warehouse) will only deal with two ISBNs—one for the plain hardcover, one for the 10-pack of cereal boxes. This is standard operating procedure for all special prepacks.

WILL WE BE ABLE TO TRACK THE EFFECT OF THE BOX ON SALES? IF A RETAILER ORDERS BOTH KINDS, CAN WE KNOW WHICH ONES ARE SELLING?
Nope.

HOW MANY CEREAL BOXES ARE WE GOING TO PRINT?
As many as you can sell in advance. And not one more.

58 **It's not about good ideas:** As long as we're talking about change, here's an astoundingly great quote from Andy Law, founder of St. Luke's ad agency, "The failure . . . was to try to simplistically replace one workable but broken system with another untried one as if a new mantra was the answer. No, the answer was to start behaving differently, to start talking differently. That way, you begin to meet other people who have been thinking along the same lines, possibly for longer and with greater application than yourself."

59 **the satisfied customers:** The same math applies to nonprofits that work so hard to satisfy today's donors, while forgoing those that they need tomorrow.

60 **That's why focus groups:** One more great thought about change: "If Henry Ford had listened to his focus groups, we would still be driving better horses" (Brian Collins, Ogilvy).

60 **Frederick's of Hollywood:** Focusing on the right issue is the best

place to start. For example, Toyota has a similar problem with the Prius. Who's going to switch to an untested car that gets fifty-five miles per gallon? I don't think it's people driving a two-year-old Corolla. Instead, I think it's people who are giving up a Miata or a Porsche or a VW Beetle. People who are trying to express themselves with their cars, and are far more likely to be unsatisfied with whatever they're currently driving (they always want something more). That ought to change the way Toyota thinks about the design and pricing of the Prius, no?

60 **my Google T-shirt:** I treasure this shirt, a gift from my friend Wes at Google.

62 **the very best vacuum cleaner:** The Dyson has a HEPA filter, no dust bag, a see-through bin for junk and a hugely powerful suck that doesn't fade over time. After I vacuumed our (clean) carpet for the first time, my wife was so disgusted by the amount of junk I had collected that she had me vacuum the whole house. And the entire family fought over taking a turn, because being powerful is . . . fun.

62 **Of course not:** Dean Kamen, the brilliant inventor, has two quotes worth sharing on this. He said, "If J. P. Morgan had said to his MBAs, 'I want to build a

railroad to the West Coast,' they would have advised against it as too capital-intensive, with an uncertain return, because the railroad would be going into nowhere. Morgan's response to such sensible MBA advice would have been, 'Morons! I know there's nothing out there. That's why I want to build the railroad!' "

Kamen also said, "Inventing is frustrating, it's dangerous, it's expensive and inventors should avoid it whenever possible. Be a systems integrator."

66 **without realizing:** The watering down I talked about is endemic. Martin Ruef, an assistant professor of organizational behavior at Stanford's Graduate School of Business did a study of Stanford alumni who started new businesses. He wanted to find out what helped them innovate. After studying nearly one thousand entrepreneurs, he came to exactly the wrong conclusion.

He concluded that the more time you spend networking (and working) with friends, the less likely you are to be creative in your work. In other words, Ruef explains, "Contrary to common assumptions, the evidence suggests that in many cases strong social ties do not provide significant new information, so it helps not to be embedded in them. . . . I found strong evidence to suggest that the longer entrepreneurs have been in the industry . . . the less innovative they are. . . . Veterans just don't come up with wacky or creative ideas that can really spark a new industry." He also concluded that people are more innovative when they're new to the industry.

I politely disagree. It's not that people somehow lose their ability to be creative when they're in an environment in which they feel safe. It's that *they ignore the creative ideas that naturally occur to them and fight the changes championed by others.*

They like things the way they are, and they can't resist the urge to defend the status quo.

The challenge of the champion is to help people who are already creative to take advantage of their talent. By selling the dream and fighting the status quo, we can free people who have been lulled into a false sense of security.

68 **precisely the same reason:** Toy companies buy plenty of ideas, but only from proven inventors, which is why you should not try to invent a toy. It'll make you crazy.

71 **based on the evidence:** I need to make my position regarding the fulcrum crystal clear: It's a little like gravity or evolution—your opinion is irrelevant. The fulcrum exists whether you believe in it

or not. I'm not saying I *want* organizations to work this way, but they do.

72   **a cool challenge:** Enrolling your peers is not that hard, especially the engineers, who get easily bored doing the same scut work day after day.

72   **make the stock price go up:** That would be, ahem, the CEO and her team. My comment about the stock price should not be ignored. Senior management with stock options tend to get pretty focused on this.

74   **your bosses look smart:** I talk about why organizations get so stuck. Understanding the fulcrum helps you understand why innovation so often happens *outside* market leaders, why companies from out of nowhere (and Silicon Valley start-ups) so often change the dynamic. When an idea doesn't require the full might and force of a huge company, it's often easier to get it done on your own.

    You only have one boss, and if she doesn't believe you can do it or that it's worth doing, you're stuck. If you can't make the fulcrum work in the eyes of that key decision maker, your work is much more difficult.

    But there are hundreds of sources of capital in the outside world, and when you approach them as an entrepreneur, you're more likely to have the posture of the champion. They *want* to believe that you're the person who can do this, and thus you're more likely to persuade them that you're the guy.

    That doesn't necessarily mean the answer is to go outside and start something new. It means, instead, that you and your boss (or your co-workers, or your employees) should sit down together and figure out which parts of the fulcrum are out of whack.

79   **"a three-blade razor!":** As I write about razors, Schick, in a rare fit of innovation, has launched a (wait for it) four-blade razor!

79   **skeumorphs:** I'm a big fan of neology which is the art of making up your own words when existing ones aren't cool enough. But no, I didn't make up *this* word. It's the art of using the known to make the unknown more palatable.

82   **Yahoo!'s domination:** Yes, that's the way we talked back then. But it's easy to forget how close this was to true. In those days, being affiliated with Yahoo! was the difference between success and failure. It was Google, times ten.

   I need to be really clear about one thing, though: Yahoo! is doing better now than ever. They're making a ton of money, growing fast and doing it reliably and doing it on schedule. Stuff I could never have imagined doing. Good for them. Nice work (if you can get it)!

86   **the champions were able:** Time to be facetious for a moment. If you're not ready to champion your idea, you can:

✳   Go to a lot of conferences.

✳   Do a lot of research.

✳   Ask for a lot of support and a big budget.

✳   Cancel a project early if the competition shows any sign of waking up.

- Cancel a project early if the competition shows no sign of waking up.

- Blame your boss, the FDA, the economy and the guys in the factory.

Of course, your idea won't launch and you'll be right where you started. The time to start is now. Hey, you're going to go to work anyway. Why not do something great while you're there?

87 **Some of the time:** Is there only one way to be a champion? Of course not. In fact, the only thing champions have in common is that they get the organization behind them and reach their goal. What follows is a wide variety of tactics . . . tactics designed to get you thinking about the fundamental principles that get an organization to do what you need it to do.

I could write a dozen books about how to organize around the idea of implementing change and innovation. If you're already a pro, go ahead and skip to the next section.

88 **"If I could persuade":** Channel conflict never goes away. Crest had this problem with Whitestrips. We all know that dentists love Crest and have made a big difference in the sales of their toothpaste. What would happen when P&G launched a product that took a big chunk of the dentists' revenue from teeth whitening services? It was unknown and untestable. Paul was smart enough to save that objection for later and answer the easy ones first.

P&G came up with two good strategies, though. First, they sold dentists on the idea that "Anything you can do to make people smile is a positive smile for dentistry." Then, Vince Hudson, the brand manager, had an insight—they let dentists have an exclusive on selling Whitestrips at the beginning of the rollout. The dentists made less per sale than they would have with custom whitening, but they sold far more patients on the idea of whitening. Today, Whitestrips are the number-one recommended whitening solution.

89 *Art and Fear:* http://www.amazon.com/exec/obidos/tg/detail/-/088 4963799/102-4412133-6209760?v=glance

91 **imprinted rubber bands:** Lobster tracking: www.islandinstitute.org. Ramit Sethi did this interview.

93 **"You work the channels":** Ramit Sethi interviewed Rich.

93 **advertising department:** Ramit Sethi interviewed Steve.

99 **new words for complicated concepts:** Here's the action item for your Web site. If you want to revamp your Web site from the useless dead end of broadband content to the more measurable, effective and profitable approach of combining ideaviruses with permission, it sure helps to measure. Measure passalong. Measure your permission asset. Once employees start asking about the stats for your pages along those measures, they're way more likely to be open to your ideas about improving the metrics!

100 **get the signature:** Ramit Sethi interviewed Bill at Starbucks.

102 **OnStar:** OnStar is a satellite-based system that helps you with navigation, service, etc. as you drive around.

106 **(and vice versa):** Some people believe that my PowerPoint riff doesn't apply to them. The work they do is too complex, they say. I got this

note the other day from Dr. Michael Freeman, who's forensic trauma epidemiologist at the Department of Public Health and Preventive Medicine at Oregon Health and Science University School of Medicine:

Dear Mr. Godin,

Someone has just sent your tutorial on bad PowerPoint presentations to me and I wanted to let you know how much I appreciated your insight. I use PowerPoint constantly for lectures worldwide (and am generally considered an excellent lecturer) but your tutorial is going to have me making some major revisions.

Unfortunately, for scientific lectures I cannot be limited to six words per slide (at least I can't figure out how this could be done).

Best wishes,

Michael Freeman

Actually, the answer is pretty simple. Even in a scientific lecture, you're trying to make a point. You're trying to persuade people that you're right and that they have something to learn. So putting line after line of bullet points on the screen is not going to work. It's not going to persuade.

The answer is to use powerful graphs (showing, for example, the percentage of people who don't have a heart attack when they take an aspirin a day) or the logos of the journals that have printed peer-reviewed articles on the topics at hand, or a photo of a healthy liver that had responded to some treatment . . .

The point is this: It doesn't matter *how* technical your topic is. It doesn't matter how dense the ideas are. If you really and truly are trying to sell people, you must do it with simple, emotional, memorable images. If the audience can't remember what you had on the screen without looking at their notes, you have failed.

109 **You never get a second chance:** Or, as my old colleague Anthony used to say, "You never get a third chance to make a second impression."

110 *Software Project Survival Guide:* If you're serious about the ideas, please click over to: http://www.amazon.com/exec/obidos/tg/detail/-/1572316217/102-4412133-6209760?v=glance. I really can't recommend this book strongly enough. If *Free Prize Inside* persuades you to read just one other book, I hope it's this one.

> 121 **the magnitude of the projects:** But don't go too far with self-censorship! My favorite Zig Ziglar story: There's this guy fishing. Across the way, he sees someone else fishing, and he's doing great. He keeps casting and then hauling in fish. But something strange is going on. Finally, our hero can't control his curiosity. He calls out, "Friend, may I ask you a question?" The successful fisherman stops and says, "Sure."
>
> "Well, I can't help but notice you're catching a lot of fish. But you keep throwing the big ones back and

> keeping the little ones. Would you mind telling me
> why you're only keeping the little tiny fish?"
>
> The fisherman pauses, looks ashamed and says,
> "Well, you know, I'd dearly love to keep the big fish,
> but all I've got is a little bitty frying pan."
>
> Please don't fool yourself into thinking you can't
> handle something important. Be realistic and you'll
> amaze yourself.

125 **(at least not at your company)**: I will share one effective tip if you decide to try brainstorming. Whenever you hear an idea that you feel like criticizing, use this phrase: "Great idea. Write it down." It allows you to move on without taking the time to criticize the factual foundation of the idea.

125 **might have to do it later**: One of the best people I ever worked with refused to brainstorm. She couldn't stop nay-saying. Finally, one day, in exasperation, I sent her home and told her not to come back to work unless she could solve the nay-saying. As soon as I said it, we both gasped. She gasped because she thought I might go through with firing her, and she needed (and liked) her job. I gasped because I felt terrible.

Best thing I ever did. She came back the next day, transformed. She turned into a great brainstormer. If you're willing to do this with your staff, it's okay with me if you try brainstorming. If you're not, forget it. (PS: My friend, when I remind her of this story, insists I've got it wrong. She decided to go for a walk on her own, I agreed not to make her brainstorm in the rigid, classical sense ever again, and we lived happily ever after. I like her version better.)

127 **even do it by yourself:** I do my edgecraft in the shower. It has the added benefit of dramatically increasing personal hygiene.

141 **how to get right to it:** When you go past the edges, you're in the fringes. The fringes aren't nearly as successful as the edges. I don't spend a lot of time in this book worrying about the fringes, because I don't believe most organizations have any idea at all how to get that far. Don't worry about it!

143 **(dwarf the competition):** *New York Times*, July 27, 2003.

143 **items, branded, would cost:** Here's how Trader Joe's engine works. They have a huge flow of people (and cash) in their stores every day. This gives them the power to go to a supplier and say, "Create this sort of chili (or chip, or fish, or whatever) and we'll buy a whole bunch. No need for you to advertise or take much risk." Not every vendor takes them up on this because their standards are high and their prices are low. But they don't need *every* vendor. They merely need enough to keep the crowds coming.

> 145 **their USP:** Unique Selling Proposition, a sixty-year-old idea that marketers use to figure out how to market something that is, in effect, average. Rosser Reeves, who developed the idea at Bates, was inducted into the Marketing Hall of Fame (I hear they have an urn waiting for me one day). This is what the hall says on its site: "Reeves believed that a basic dilemma in

> advertising was that few products were distinctly different. Reeves developed the USP concept in an attempt to distinguish one product from its competitors. The USP was an advancement over previous 'reason-why' advertising in that it operated as a part of consumer identity. The USP was similar to, but different from, David Ogilvy's brand imagery." Just to share my favorite example, the USP of Gleem toothpaste: "For people who are too busy to brush after every meal." I don't make this stuff up.
>
> Sort of the antiprize. I say, if your product is not distinctly different, don't come up with better ads. Come up with a better product!

146 **little photo books:** http://club.nokia.co.jp/tokyoq/tokyoscape/puri01 .html

147 **(Hallmark cards):** The Nathan's contest was covered at length by *The New York Times Magazine*, and thousands watch it every year. Hallmark, of course, succeeds because the person who buys a card then markets the company by sending that card to a friend!

147 **likely that people will:** *Unleashing the Ideavirus* was all about this edge. You can find free copies online (search for "download ideavirus" in Google) or you can get a copy at a local bookstore.

148 **extraordinary pipette:** http://www.frogdesign.com/design/product/ id/vistalab/

151 **dealership in Delaware:** http://www.mikesfamous.com/

152 **three flavors of milkshakes:** Of course, In-N-Out also does something even more remarkable. They have a secret menu! A menu not posted that only insiders know about, which makes it fun to take neophytes there and share the secret. For those who can't bear the fact that there's a secret they're not party to, here's the official company line: "We have several commonly requested burger styles, such as Animal-style, which do not appear on our menu. As you may know, our Animal-style burgers come with lettuce, tomato, extra spread, pickles, grilled onions, and mustard fried into the patty. We also offer Protein-style burgers, for which we wrap the burger in large leaves of lettuce instead of placing it on a bun.

"In addition, we have commonly requested burgers that are not on our menu. These burgers include the Wish burger, the Grilled Cheese burger, the Double-Meat, and the 3x3. The Wish burger is similar to a hamburger but does not contain the meat. The Grilled Cheese burger is similar to the Wish burger, but adds two slices of melted cheese. The Double-Meat is similar to the Double-Double in that it has two meat patties, but it does not have cheese. The 3x3 burger is a burger with three meat patties and three slices of cheese, and you can add meat patties and slices of cheese to make a 4x4, 5x5, etc."

152 **Jesse James:** http://www.fortune.com/fortune/smallbusiness/articles/0,15114,427131,00.html

155 **caters to fat people:** http://www.signonsandiego.com/news/mexico/20030607-0957-beachforthebig.html

155 **Minnesota Typeface Competition:** You can try it at http://design.umn.edu:8080/cgi-bin/ltrstr/tcdc/alternator?page=interface_004

Keith's Three-Step Process

1. DEFINE THE PROBLEM

- Defining the problem

- Envisioning the end state (knowing what victory looks like)

- Defining the approach by which victory can be achieved

- Inciting support and then action

2. INNOVATING

- Seeking insight to inform the prototyping of the solution

- Prototyping potential solutions

- Delineating the tough choices

- Enabling the team to work as a team

3. GENERATING VALUE

- Choosing the best solution, then activating it

- Making sure people know about your solution

- Selling the solution

> • Rapidly learning and "tacking" based on your successes and failures

158 **what great design can do:** Marcia Hart is an architect who understands organizational design. She can tell, with a glance at a company's phone directory, how well the place is run. By redesigning an organization the way she designs a building, she delivers nearly instant results.

158 **completely sold out for months:** http://haeftling.de/index.html

163 **Peace Frogs:** http://www.peacefrogs.com/insideEntrepreneurs.php

169 **Archie McPhee:** www.archiemcphee.com

170 **outlets in museums:** The chocolate exhibit at the Museum of Natural History seemed to have one objective: to give them an excuse to sell you chocolate bars on the way out!

170 **on airplanes:** Interesting fact about this: An airline can double their profit on a cheap ticket if they can sell you a watch or perfume on the flight. Once the plane is flying anyway, many airlines are willing to fly the last passenger for a tiny profit above marginal cost. The $40 profit on a cheap watch is more than enough to double that.

171 **Joi Ito does:** http://joi.ito.com

172 **a boom in sales:** http://sfgate.com/cgi-bin/article.cgi?file=/chronicle/archive/2003/04/16/HO119693.DTL

175 **a photo link:** http://customerevangelists.typepad.com/blog/2003/09/cnn_in_the_show.html

175 **Holiday Inn billow:** There have been scientific studies done on precisely why the shower curtain blows in on you. Visit http://slashdot.org/science/01/07/15/1355250.shtml for details.

182 **make something happen!:** My last thought is about old and new:

The old way is the way you remember: Make a product. An average product for average people. Manufacture the product. Get distribution. Run ads. Run more ads. Sell the product. Buy more ads. Reduce costs. Sell the product. Repeat.

The new way feels trickier because I've been busy making up a lot of new words to capture the essence of it (I know, all these terms do look a little ridiculous, especially strung together, but bear with me). It's like this:

Make something remarkable. Create a Purple Cow with a free prize inside. Create a fashion. Get sneezers excited about your product, help it become an ideavirus within a hive. Get permission from the early adopters with otaku, so you can keep in touch with them and let them know about your *next* fashionable soft innovation. Milk the cow, make a profit. Use edgecraft to make your next free prize. Alert the permission base of sneezers. Repeat.

INDEX

BULL MARKET

500 Writers, Designers, Inventors, Prototypers, Suppliers and Resources That Can Help You Create A Purple Cow

Yes, a free prize inside a book called *Free Prize Inside*. What did you expect?

Get this 500-page eBook (a $21 value) as my gift to you.

Your free prize for buying this book.

Visit www.freeprizeinside.com/bullmarket123

Free Prize Inside!, Condensed

Every company needs to grow, and traditionally, organizations have focused on two reliable ways to accomplish that growth: big ads and big innovation.

Big ads are a problem because advertising doesn't work like it used to. Many ads are underwater, costing more than they generate.

Big innovation is a problem too. R&D is too expensive, and the glut of technology and patents and noise makes it harder than ever to predict and then successfully execute the next big thing.

Fortunately, there's a third way. Soft innovations. The clever, insightful, useful small ideas that just about anyone in an organization can think up. Soft innovations can make your product into a Purple Cow; they can make it remarkable. They do this by solving a problem that's peripheral to what your product is ostensibly about. It's a second reason to buy the thing, and perhaps a first reason to talk about it. It may seem like a gimmick, but soon, what seems like a gimmick becomes an essential element in your product or service.

I call this sort of innovation (when it succeeds) a free prize, because the revenue associated with it is far greater than the cost of implementing it.

Finding a free prize isn't the difficult part. The difficult part is getting the rest of the organization to embrace it. The only way that can possibly occur is if someone becomes a champion for the idea.

Championing an idea is essential, but no one ever taught us how to do it. By adopting the posture of the champion and following in the path of those who have successfully done it in the past, you can learn how to make something happen.

Every champion has her own range. It's a mistake to try to champion much beyond your reach. Picking a free prize that you can actually execute is much smarter than picking the "best" free prize.

Finding the free prize doesn't involve brainstorming. Instead, use edgecraft. Edgecraft is an iterative process that is much easier for an organization to embrace than brainstorming.

There are hundreds of available edges, things you can add to, subtract from or otherwise change about your product or service. Find an edge and go all the way to it. Going partway is time-consuming and expensive—and it doesn't work very well.

Going all the way to the edge is the only way to jolt the user into noticing what you've done. If they notice you, they're one step closer to talking about you.

It's all marketing now. The organizations that win will be the ones that realize that all they must do is create things worth talking about.

THE NEXT BIG MARKETING IDEA

So, the future belongs to people who can invent, implement and sell the ideas—the free prizes—that become Purple Cows. It sounds daunting, but it's not.

First step: Realize that it's *all* marketing. The only reason for all the effort of all the people in your organization is to spread the word—your word. Free-prize thinking is a way to formalize that.

Second step: Do it out loud. Tell other people what you're up to. Do it together.

Third step: Get help. Ad agencies won't be ad agencies much longer. They're itching to walk into your organization and help your people make remarkable stuff. The free book *Bull Market* (see page 233) will give you a head start in finding the help you need.

Just start. Start now. Fail often. Enjoy the ride.